Y0-BTA-645

AutoCAD Release 13 Update Guide

(For DOS and Windows)

AutoCAD Release 13
Update Guide
(For DOS and Windows)

Sham Tickoo

Associate Professor
Department of Manufacturing Engineering Technologies
and Supervision
Purdue University Calumet
Hammond, Indiana

DEDICATION
To teachers, who make it possible to disseminate knowledge to enlighten the young and curious minds of our future generations

To students, who are dedicated to learning new technologies and making the world a better place to live

Thanks
To the faculty and students of the METS department of Purdue University Calumet for their cooperation.

Delmar Publishers

1945 - 1995

I(T)P™
An International Thomson Publishing Company

Albany • Bonn • Boston • Cincinnati • Detroit • London • Madrid
Melbourne • Mexico City • New York • Pacific Grove • Paris • San Francisco
Singapore • Tokyo • Toronto • Washington

ENG /
.07468052

NOTICE TO THE READER

Publisher does not warrant or guarantee any of the products described herein or perform any independent analysis in connection with any of the product information contained herein. Publisher does not assume, and expressly disclaims, any obligation to obtain and include information other than that provided to it by the manufacturer.

The reader is expressly warned to consider and adopt all safety precautions that might be indicated by the activities herein and to avoid all potential hazards. By following the instructions contained herein, the reader willingly assumes all risks in connection with such instructions.

The publisher makes no representation or warranties of any kind, including but not limited to, the warranties of fitness for particular purpose or merchantability, nor are any such representations implied with respect to the material set forth herein, and the publisher takes no responsibility with respect to such material. The publisher shall not be liable for any special, consequential, or exemplary damages resulting, in whole or part, from the readers' use of, or reliance upon, this material.

Trademarks
AutoCAD® and the AutoCAD® logo are registered trademarks of Autodesk, Inc.
Windows is a trademark of the Microsoft Corporation.
All other product names are acknowledge as trademarks of their respective owners.

Cover Design:Michael Speke

Delmar Staff
Publisher: Michael McDermott
Acquisitions Editor: Mary Beth Ray, CompuServe 73234,3664
Project Development Editor: Jenna Daniels, CompuServe 76433,1677
Production Coordinator: Andrew Crouth, CompuServe 74507,250
Art and Design Coordinator: Lisa L. Bower

COPYRIGHT © 1996
By Delmar Publishers Inc.
an International Thomson Publishing Company
The ITP logo is a trademark under license.

Printed in the United States of America

For more information, contact:

Delmar Publishers
3 Columbia Circle, Box 15015
Albany, New York 12212-5015

International Thomson Publishing Europe
Berkshire House 168-173
High Holborn
London, WC1V 7AA
England

Thomas Nelson Australia
102 Dodds Street
South Melbourne, 3205
Victoria, Australia

Nelson Canada
1120 Birchmont Road
Scarborough, Ontario
Canada, M1K 5G4

International Thomson Editores
Campos Eliseos 385, Piso 7
Col Polanco
11560 Mexico D F Mexico

International Thomson Publishing GmbH
Konigswinterer Strasse 418
53227 Bonn
Germany

International Thomson Publishing Asia
221 Henderson Road
#05-10 Henderson Building
Singapore 0315

International Thomson Publishing--Japan
Hirakawacho Kyowa Building, 3F
2-2-1 Hirakawacho
Chiyoda-ku, Tokyo 102
Japan

All rights reserved. No part of this work covered by the copyright hereon may be reproduced or used in any form or by any means—graphic, electronic, or mechanical, including photocopying, recording, taping, or information storage and retrieval systems—without the written permission of the publisher.

1 2 3 4 5 6 7 8 9 10 XXX 00 99 98 97 96 95

Tickoo, Sham
AutoCAD Release 13 Update Guide (for DOS and Windows)

ISBN: 0-8273-7433-X

Table of Contents

T385
T5244
1996
ENGI

7

Introduction

AutoCAD Release 13 represents a major advance that has made AutoCAD very flexible and efficient. New commands have been added and some existing commands have been updated to make it easier to edit objects, dimensions, and text. The user interface has been significantly improved to allow increased user access. AutoCAD now supports International Standards Organization (ISO) drawing specifications. Also, the on-line tutorials, on-line help, and documentation have made it easier to learn AutoCAD.

This guide, written for those who wish to become familiar with the enhancements and commands new to AutoCAD Release 13, contains a detailed description of the new features. The commands have been grouped based on their functionality, which makes it easier for the user to locate and understand the function and application of the commands. At the end of each major topic, there is an example that illustrates the function of the command and how it can be used in the drawing. At the end of most chapters, there are exercises that can be used to apply the skills just learned. Please refer to the following table for conventions used in this guide.

Convention	Example
Command names appear capitalized	the MOVE command
Screen menu names appear capitalized	screen menu DRAW1
Pull-down menu names appear with the first letter capitalized	pull-down menu Draw
A key icon appears when you should respond by striking ENTER	↵
Command sequences are indented. Responses are indicated by boldface. Directions are indicated by italics or are enclosed in parentheses.	Command: **MOVE** Select Objects: **G** Enter group name: *Enter group name*

Also Available from Delmar Publishers...

AutoCAD: A Problem Solving Approach

by

Sham Tickoo

AutoCAD: A Problem Solving Approach features detailed explanations of AutoCAD Release 13 commands and how to use them in solving drafting and design problems. This book is both a comprehensive introduction to AutoCAD Release 13 and a tool for sharpening your problem-solving skills. Every AutoCAD Release 13 command is thoroughly explained with examples, illustrations, and application problems from a variety of sources. Armed with this book, you will gain the knowledge and confidence you need to use AutoCAD Release 13 to tackle drafting and design challenges. The following are some of the features of this book.

1. Step-by-step explanations to take you through every AutoCAD Release 13 command.

2. Coverage of basic drafting and design concepts such as orthographic projections, dimensioning principles, sectioning, auxiliary views, detail, and assembly drawings provides users with the essential drafting skills they need to solve drawing problems with AutoCAD Release 13.

3. The customizing section of **AutoCAD: A Problem Solving Approach** covers the following topics:
   Creating prototype drawings
   Writing script files and creating slide shows
   Creating new linetypes and hatch patterns
   Creating shapes and text fonts
   Writing screen, tablet, pull-down, cascading, cursor, image button, and auxiliary menus
   Writing DIESEL, string expression language macros to customize the status line
   Editing ACAD.PGP files

4. **AutoCAD: A Problem Solving Approach** covers AutoLISP functions and their application in writing programs and editing drawing database.

5. **AutoCAD: A Problem Solving Approach** also introduces the user to Dialogue Control Language and how to use this language to create dialogue boxes.

6. **AutoCAD: A Problem Solving Approach** contains a detailed description of paper space, geometry calculator, paragraph text, multilines, complex linetypes, 3D drawings, solid modeling, and rendering.

OBJECT GROUPING (GROUP Command)

You can use the group command to group AutoCAD objects and assign a name to the group. Once you have created the groups, you can select the objects by group name. The individual characteristics of an object are not effected by forming groups. Groups is simply a mechanism that enables the user to form groups and edit the objects by groups. It makes the object selection process easier and faster. The objects can be a member of several groups. Although, an object belongs to a group, you can still select an object as if it did not belong to any group. Groups can be selected by entering the group name or by selecting an object that belongs to the group. You can also highlight the objects in a group or sequentially highlight the groups an object belongs to. You invoke the **Object Grouping** dialogue box from the screen menu (Select ASSIST/ Group), pull-down menu (Select Assist/ Group Objects...), or by entering **GROUP** at AutoCAD's Command: prompt.

    Command: GROUP

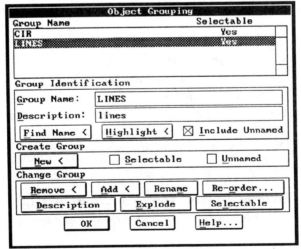

Figure 1-1 Object Grouping dialogue box

You can also use the GROUP command from the Command line by entering -**GROUP** (dash followed by GROUP) at the Command: prompt. In AutoCAD for Windows use the tilde symbol (~**GROUP**).

    Command: ~GROUP
    ?/Order/Add/Remove/Selectable < Make > :

The Object Grouping dialogue box provides the following options:

1

Group Name

The Group Name area of the Object Grouping dialogue box displays the names of the existing groups.

Group Identification

Group Name:

The **Group Name:** edit box displays the name of the existing or selected group. You can also use **Group Name:** edit box to enter the name of the new group. You can enter any name, but it is recommended to use the names that reflect the type of entities in the group. For example, the group name "LINES" can include all lines and a group name "Attributes" can include all attribute definitions. The group names can be up to 31 characters long and can include special characters ($, _, and -). The group names can have any spaces.

Description:

The **Description:** edit box displays the description of the existing or the selected group. It can be used to enter the description of the group. The length of the description text can be up to 64 characters, including spaces.

Find Name

The **Find Name:** button is used to find the group name/names associated with an object. When you select this button, AutoCAD will prompt you to select the object. Once you select the object, the dialogue box will appear on the screen displaying the group names that the selected object belongs to.

Figure 1-2 Group Member List dialogue box

Highlight

The **Highlight:** button is used to highlight the objects that are in the selected group name. The group name can be selected by picking the group name in the Group Names list box at the top of the dialogue box.

Include Unnamed

The **Include Unnamed** button is used to display the names of the unnamed objects in the "Object Grouping" dialogue box. The unnamed groups are created when you copy a named object. AutoCAD automatically assigns a name to the copied objects. The format of the name is Ax (For example *A1, *A2, *A3, ...). If you select the Include Unnamed button, the unnamed object names (*A1, *A2, *A3, ...) will be displayed in the dialogue box. The unnamed groups can also be created by not assigning a name to the group (See **unnamed** in Create Group section).

Create Group

New

The **New** button is used to define a new group, after you have entered the group name in the Group Name: edit box. Once you select the **New** button, the dialogue box will temporarily disappear and AutoCAD will prompt you to select objects. After selecting the objects, the dialogue box will reappear on the screen.

Selectable

The **Selectable** button allows the user to define a group that is selectable. By doing so, the user can select the entire group when one object in the group is selected. The following example illustrates the use of this option.

Command: **ERASE**
Select objects: CTRL+A *(Press the CTRL and A keys)*
<Groups on>: *Select an object that belongs to a group (If the group has been defined as selectable, all entities belonging to that group will be selected.)*

The group selection can also be turned on or off from the pull-down menu (Select Assist/ Group Selection). The Group Selection is on if a check mark is displayed in front of the Group Selection item in the Assist pull-down menu. If the group is not defined as selectable, you cannot select all objects in the group, even if you turn the group on by pressing the **Ctrl** and **A** keys.

Note

The combination of Ctrl and A keys is used as a toggle key to turn the group selection on or off. If the group selection is off (<Groups off>), the group selection is disabled.

Unnamed

When you create a group, you can assign it a name or leave it unnamed. If you select Unnamed, AutoCAD will automatically assign a group name to the selected objects. The format of the name is Ax (*A1, *A2, *A3, ...), where x is incremented with each new unnamed group.

Change Group

Remove

The **Remove** button is used to remove entities from the selected group. Once you select the group name from the Group Names list box and then select the Remove button, the dialogue box will temporarily disappear and AutoCAD will display the following prompt on the screen:

Remove
Select objects to remove:
Remove objects: *Select objects*   *(Select objects that you want to remove from the selected group)*

If you remove all objects from the group, the group name still exists, unless you use the Explode option to remove the group definition (See Explode in Change Group section).

Add

The **Add** button is used to add entities to the selected group. When you select this option, AutoCAD will prompt you to select the objects that you want to add to the selected group. The prompt sequence is similar to Remove option.

Rename

The **Rename** button is used to rename the selected group. To rename a group, first you select the group name from the Group Names list box and then enter the name in the Group Name: edit box. Now, select the Rename button and AutoCAD will rename the specified group.

Re-order

The **Re-order** option lets you change the order of the objects in the selected group. The objects are numbered in the order in which you pick them when selecting objects for the group. Sometimes, when creating a tool path, you may want to change the order of these objects to get a continuous tool motion. This can be accomplished by using the Re-order option. When you select the Reorder button, AutoCAD displays the **Order Group** dialogue box. The following example illustrates the use of this dialogue box:

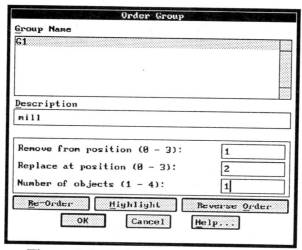

Figure 1-3 Order Group dialogue box

Example 1

The drawing of Figure 1-4 shows four objects that are in group G1. Determine the order of these objects and then reorder the objects in clockwise direction.

1. Invoke the **Object Grouping** dialogue box and make the group (G1) current by selecting it from the Group Name list box.

2. Pick the Re-order button from the dialogue box, **Order Group** dialogue box is displayed on the screen. Select the group G1, if not already selected.

3. Use the Highlight button to highlight the individual objects in the selected group. You can use the Next and Previous buttons to cycle through the group objects. Figure 1-4 (a) shows the order of the objects in group G1. To create a tool path so that the tool moves in a clockwise direction, it is necessary to re-order the objects as shown in Figure 1-4(b).

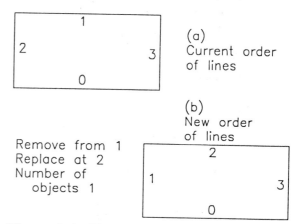

Figure 1-4 Changing the order of group objects

4. To get a clockwise tool path, we must switch object numbers 1 and 2. This can be accomplished by entering the necessary information in the **Order Group** dialogue box. Enter 1 in the **Remove from position** edit box and 2 in the **Replace at position** edit box. Enter 1 in the **Number of objects** edit box, since there is only one object to be replaced.

5. After entering the information, select the Re-Order button to re-order the objects. You can confirm the change by selecting the Highlight button again and cycling through the objects.

6. If you want to reverse the order of the objects in the group, select the Reverse Order button.

Description

The **Description** button lets the user change the description of the selected group. To change the description of a group, first you select the group name from the Group Names list box and then enter the new description in the Description: edit box. Now, select the Description button and AutoCAD will update the description of the specified group. The description cannot exceed 64 characters, including spaces.

Explode

The **Explode** option deletes group definition of the selected group. The objects that were in the group become regular entities without a group reference.

Selectable

The **Selectable** button changes the selectable status of the selected group. To change the selectable status of the group, first select the group name from the Group Names list box and then pick the Selectable button. If the selectable status is "yes", the user can select the entire group when one object in the group is selected. If the selectable status is "no", you cannot select the entire group by selecting one object in the group.

SELECTING GROUPS

A group can be selected by selecting Group option from the pull-down menu (Select Assist/ Select objects/ Group) or by entering **G** at the AutoCAD prompt **Select Objects:**

Example
Command: **MOVE**
Select objects: **G**
Enter group name: *Enter group name*
4 found
Select objects: ◄─┘

In the Assist pull-down menu, if you select Group Objects, it invokes the Object Grouping dialogue box. Also, if you select Group Selection, it turns the group selection on or off. A check mark designates that the Group Selection is on, otherwise it is off.

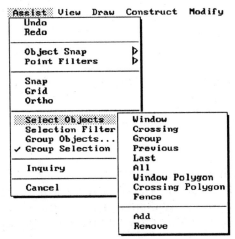

Figure 1-5 Selecting the Group option from the pull-down menu

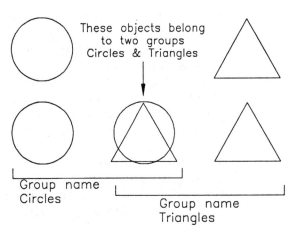

Figure 1-6 Object Selection Cycling

OBJECT SELECTION CYCLING

Cycling Through Groups

When you use the GROUP command to form object groups, AutoCAD lets you sequentially highlight the groups of which the selected object is a member. For example, let us assume that an object belongs to two different groups and you want to highlight the objects in those groups. To accomplish this, press the CTRL key at the **Select objects:** prompt and select the object that belongs to different groups. AutoCAD will highlight the objects in one of the groups and to cycle through the groups press the pick button of your pointing device. The following example illustrates this process:

Command: **ERASE**
Select objects: *Press and hold down the CTRL key*
< Cycle on >: *Select the object that belongs to different groups*
(Press the pick button on your pointing device to cycle through the groups)
Select objects: ←┘

Cycling Through Objects

You can also use the CTRL key to cycle through the objects that intersect at a point. For example, if there are several lines intersecting at a point and you want to select a particular line. You can cycle through the lines by using the intersection object snap and then holding down the CTRL key and picking a point. The following example illustrates the object selection cycling. In this example it is assumed that the lines are intersecting at a point.

Command: **ERASE**
Select objects: **INT** ←┘
of
                                    (Press the CTRL key and hold it down, select the intersection point)
< Cycle on >:
                                    (You can cycle through the objects intersecting at that point by pressing the pick button on the pointing device. Once you find the desired object, press the Enter key)

Select object: ←┘

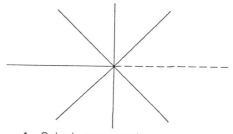

1. Select command
2. Select INT O'Snap
3. Press and hold down Ctrl. key and select intersection point
4. Click the pick button to cycle through the objects

Figure 1-7 Object selection cycling

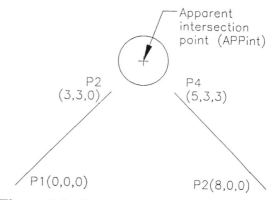

Figure 1-8 Using APParent intersection (APPint) object snap

T385, T5244   1996

ap to the apparent intersection of two coplanar or
ntersect. The following figure show two 3D lines
mmand prompt sequence for drawing a circle with
given lines:

-1. Assume the missing dimensions.
G1 that includes all lines and the slot. Description

of group G1.
m the group G1.
-Post.

bjects that belong to group New-Post.
t the Include Unnamed check box. Notice that

group has been added to the list.

9. Use the add option to add Post-2 to group New-Post.
10 Make a copy of the group New-Post to get Post-3 and Post-4.

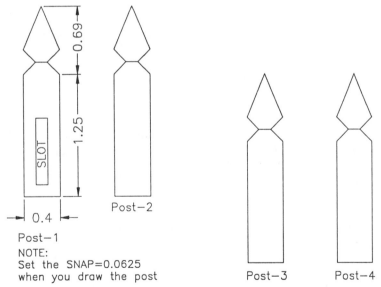

Post-1
NOTE:
Set the SNAP=0.0625
when you draw the post

Post-2

Post-3   Post-4

Figure 1-9 Drawing for Exercise

2

Edit Commands

LENGTHEN

Like TRIM and EXTEND commands, the **LENGTHEN** command can be used to extend or shorten the lines. The LENGTHEN command has several options that allow the user to change the length of entities by dynamically dragging the object endpoint, entering delta value, entering percentage value, or by entering total length of the object. The lengthen command also allows repeated selection of objection for editing. The lengthen command does not have any effect on closed object like circle.

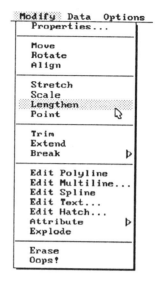

Figure 2-1 Selecting LENGTHEN command from the pull-down menu

Command: **LENGTHEN**
DElta/Percent/Total/DYnamic/ < Select object > :

< Select object >

This is the default option that returns the length or angle of the selected object. If the object is a line, AutoCAD only returns length. However, if the selected object is an arc, AutoCAD returns the length and angle.

DElta

The **DElta** option is used to increase or decrease the length or angle of an object by defining the delta distance or delta angle. The delta value can be entered by entering a numerical value or by picking two points. A positive value will increase (Extend) the length of the selected object and a negative value will decrease the length (Trim). The following is the command prompt sequence for decreasing the angle of an arc by 30 degrees.

Command: **LENGTHEN**
DElta/Percent/Total/DYnamic/ < Select object > : **DE**
Angle/ < Enter delta length (default) > : **A**
Enter delta angle < default > : **-30**
< Select object to change > /Undo: Select object
< Select object to change > /Undo: ◄─┘

Percent

The **Percent** option is used to extend or trim an object by defining the change as a percentage of the original length of angle. For example, a positive number of 150 will increase the length by 50 percent and a positive number of 75 will decrease the length of angle by 25 percent of the original value. (Negative values are not allowed).

8

Total

The **Total** option is used to extend or trim an object by defining the new total length or angle. For example, if you enter total length of 1.25, AutoCAD will automatically increase or decrease the length of the object so that the new length of the object is 1.25. The value can be entered by entering a numerical value or by picking two points. The object is shortened or lengthened with respect to the endpoint that is closest to the selection point. The selection point is determined by where the object was selected.

DYnamic

The **DYnamic** option allows the user to dynamically change the length or angle of an object by picking one of the endpoints and dragging it to a new location. The other end of the object stays fixed and is not effected by dragging.

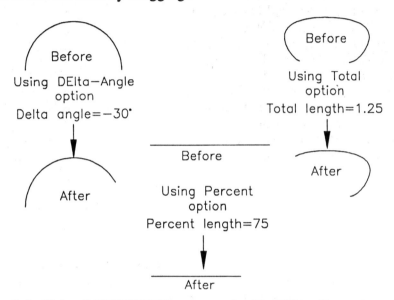

Figure 2-2 Using LENGTHEN command with DElta, Percent, and Total options

TRIM AND EXTEND ENHANCEMENTS

The trim and extend commands can be used with text, region or spline as edges. This makes the trim and extend command one of the most useful editing commands in AutoCAD. The TRIM and EXTEND command can also be used with splines, ellipses, 3D Pline, Ray and Xline.

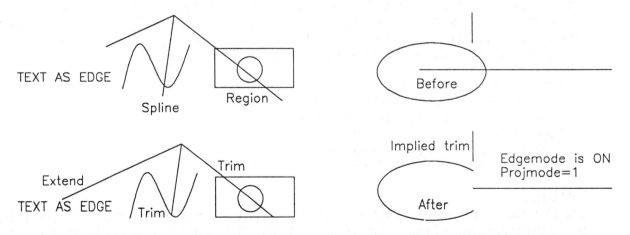

Figure 2-3 Using TRIM and EXTEND commands with text, spline, and region

Figure 2-4 Using implied trim without declared edge

The system variables **PROJMODE** and **EDGEMODE** determine how the TRIM and EXTEND commands are executed. The PROJMODE variable is saved with the drawing file, EXTEDGE variable is not. The following is the list of the values that can be assigned to these variables.

Value	PROJMODE	EDGEMODE
0	True 3D mode	Use regular edge without extension (default)
1	Project to current UCS XY plane (default)	Extend the edge to natural boundary
2	Project to current view plane	

FILLET ENHANCEMENTS

Capping

FILLET command can also be used to cap the ends of two parallel lines. The cap is a semicircle whose radius is equal to half the distance between the two parallel lines. The cap distance, radius of the semicircle, is automatically calculated when you select the two parallel lines for filleting. The CHAMFER command also lets you create a chamfer between the objects that do not lie on the current UCS. The FILLET command can be invoked from the pull-down menu (Select Construct/ Fillet), screen menu (Select CONSTRUCT/ Fillet:), or by entering the FILLET command at AutoCAD's Command: prompt.

Command: **FILLET**
(Trim mode) Current fillet radius = 0.0000
Polyline/Radius/Trim <Select first object>:

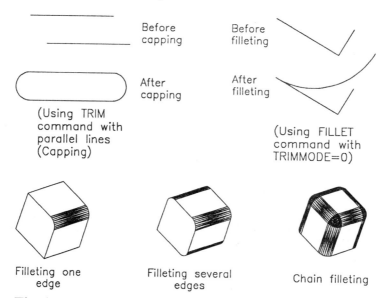

Figure 2-5 Capping parallel lines with fillet command, filleting without cutting the geometry, filleting polylines.

Trimmode

Trimmode is a system variable that eliminates any size restriction on the FILLET command. By setting Trimmode to 0, you can create a fillet of any size without actually cutting the existing geometry. Also, there is no restriction on the fillet radius, the fillet radius can be larger than one or both objects that are being filleted. The value of the Trimmode system variable can be set by entering TRIMMODE at AutoCAD's Command: prompt:

Command: **TRIMMODE**
New value for TRIMMODE <1>: **0**

Note

TRIMMODE = 0   *Fillet or Chamfer without cutting the existing geometry.*
TRIMMODE = 1   *Will extend or trim the geometry*

When you enter the FILLET command, AutoCAD displays the current Trimmode and the current fillet radius.

You cannot trim different plolylines or polyline arcs

You can also change the trim mode with **FILLET** command by selecting the Trim option as follows:

Command: **FILLET**
(NOTRIM mode) Current fillet radius = **0.2500**
Polyline/Radius/Trim/<Select first object>: **T**
Trim/No trim <No trim>: **T**
Polyline/Radius/Trim/<Select first object>: **T**

Filleting Entities with Different UCS

The fillet command will also fillet the entities that are not in the plane of current UCS. To create fillet for such entities, AutoCAD will automatically change the UCS transparently so that it can generate a fillet between the selected entities.

CREATING CHAMFER

The **CHAMFER** command allows you to create a chamfer between two objects by defining the two chamfer distances (CHAMFERC and CHAMFERD) or the length of the chamfer and the angle that the chamfer makes with the first object. The Trim option lets you set the trimmode. When you enter the CHAMFER command, AutoCAD displays the current Trimmode setting and current chamfer parameters. The CHAMFER command also lets you create a chamfer between the objects that do not lie on the current UCS. The CHAMFER command can be invoked from the pull-down menu (Select Construct/ Chamfer), screen menu (Select CONSTRUCT/ Chamfer:), or by entering the CHAMFER command at AutoCAD's Command: prompt.

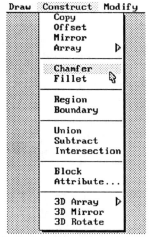

Figure 2-6 Selecting Chamfer command from the pull-down menu

Command: **CHAMFER**
(Trim mode) Current chamfer Dist1=0.1500, Dist2=0.1500
Polyline/Distance/Angle/Trim/Method/<Select first line>:

CHAMFER Command Options

Polyline

You can use the **Polyline** option to chamfer a 2D polyline. After you specify the chamfer distances and select the polyline, AutoCAD creates a chamfer between the intersecting polyline segments as shown in Figure 2-7(b).

Command: **CHAMFER**
Polyline/Distance/Angle/Trim/Method/ < Select first line > : **P**
Select 2D polyline: *Select polyline*

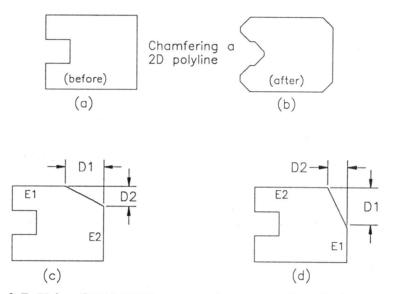

Figure 2-7 Using CHAMFER command to create chamfer between two lines or polyline segments.

Distance

The **Distance** option lets you define the chamfer distances from the selected edges. The first distance (Dist1) is assigned to the first selected edge and the second distance (Dist2) is assigned to the second edge, Figure 2-8(c) & (d). Therefore, the order in which you select the edges for creating a chamfer is important. After you specify the chamfer distances, use the CHAMFER command again to create a chamfer between two selected line segments.

Command: **CHAMFER**
Polyline/Distance/Angle/Trim/Method/ < Select first line > : **D**
Enter first chamfer distance < current > : *Enter Dist 1*
Enter second chamfer distance < current > : *Enter Dist 2*

Note

If Dist 1 and Dist 2 are set to zero, the CHAMFER command will extend or trim the selected lines so that they end at the same point.

Angle

The Angle option lets you create a chamfer by specifying length and the chamfer angle, Figure 2-8(a).

Command: **CHAMFER**
Polyline/Distance/Angle/Trim/Method/ < select first line > : **A**
Enter chamfer length on the first line < 0.500 > : *Enter chamfer length*

Enter chamfer angle from the first line < 45.0000 > : *Enter chamfer angle*

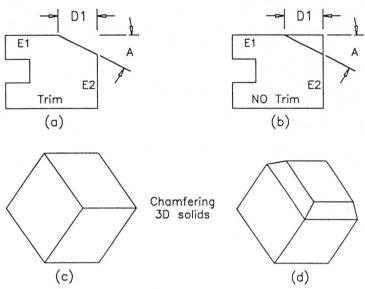

Figure 2-8 Using chamfer command to create chamfer

Trim

The setting of Trim mode determines whether AutoCAD trims the selected edges. If case of Trim, the edges will be trimmed and in case of No Trim the edges that are chamfered will not be trimmed, Figure 2-8(b)

Command: **CHAMFER**
Polyline/Distance/Angle/Trim/Method/ < select first line > : **T**
Trim/No Trim < current > : *Enter T or N*
Distance/Angle < current > : *Enter D or A*

Method

The **Method** option can be used to select the distance-distance or the distance-angle option for creating a chamfer.

Command: **CHAMFER**
Polyline/Distance/Angle/Trim/Method/ < select first line > : **M**
Distance/Angle < current > : *Enter D or A*

SETTING CHAMFER SYSTEM VARIABLE

The Chamfer modes can also be set by using the following system variable:

CHAMMODE = 0	Distance/Distance (default)
CHAMMODE = 1	Length/Angle
CHAMFERC	Sets the chamfer distance on the first selected line (default = 0)
CHAMFERD	Sets the chamfer angle from the first line (default = 0)

Exercise

First draw the figure as shown at the top and then use the FILLET, CHAMFER, and TRIM commands to obtain the figure as shown in the bottom drawing (Figure 2-9). (Set the SNAP=0.05. Also, assume the missing dimensions)

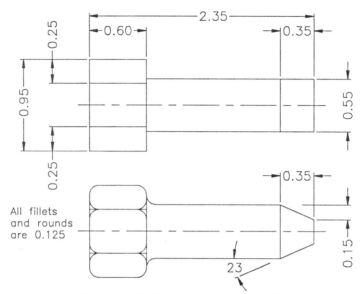

Figure 2-9 Drawing for Exercise

3 Draw Commands

DRAWING CONSTRUCTION LINES
(XLINE and RAY Command)

The XLINE and RAY commands can be used to draw construction or projection lines. XLINE is a 3D line that extends to infinity on both ends. Since the line is infinite in length, it does not have any endpoints. A RAY is a 3D line that extends to infinity only on one end. The other end of the ray has a finite endpoint.

The Xlines and Rays have zero extents. This means that the extents of the drawing will not change if you use the commands, like ZOOM command with All option, that change the drawing extents. Most of the object snap modes work with both Xlines and Rays with some limitations. You cannot use the endpoint object snap with the Xline because by definition an Xline does not have any endpoints. However, for Rays you can use the endpoint snap on one end only. Also, the Xlines and Rays take the properties of the layer in which they are drawn. The linetype will be continuous even if the linetype assigned to the layer is not continuous.

XLINE Options

<From Point>
If you select the default option, AutoCAD will prompt you to select two point, From point: and Through point:. After you select the first point, AutoCAD will dynamically rotate the Xline with the cursor. When you select the second point, Xline will be created that passes through the first point and the second point.

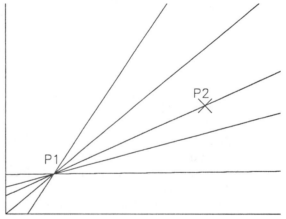

Figure 3-1 Using Angular option to draw Xlines

```
Command: XLINE
Hor/Ver/Ang/Bisect/Offset/<From point>: Specify a point
Through point: Specify the second point
```

Horizontal
The **Horizontal** option will create horizontal Xlines of infinite length that will pass through the selected points. The Xlines will be parallel to the X axis of the current UCS.

Vertical
The **Vertical** option will create vertical Xlines of infinite length that will pass through the selected points. The Xlines will be parallel to the Y axis of the current UCS.

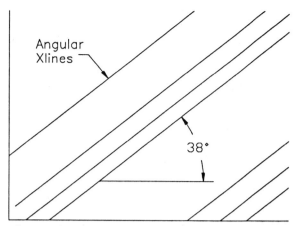

Figure 3-2 Using Horizontal and Vertical option to draw Xlines

Figure 3-3 Using Angular option to draw Xlines

Angular

The **Angular** option will create Xlines of infinite length that will pass through the selected point at a specified angle. The angle can be specified by entering a value from the keyboard or using the reference option to select an object and then referencing the angle with the selected line. The following is the command prompt sequence for reference option:

Command: **XLINE**
Hor/Ver/Ang/Bisect/Offset/ < From Point > : **Ang**
Reference/ < Enter angle (0.0000) > : **R**
Select a line object: Select a line
Enter angle < 0.0000 > : Enter angle   *(The angle will be measured with respect to the selected line. If the angle is 0, the Xlines will be parallel to the selected line)*

Bisect

The **Bisect** option will create an Xline that passes through the angle vertex and bisects an angle. The angle is specified by selecting two points. The Xline created by using this option will lie in the plane defined by the selected points. You could use the object snaps to pick the points on the existing entities. The following is the command prompt sequence for this option:

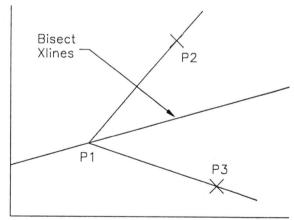

Figure 3-4 Using Bisect option to draw a Xline

Command: **XLINE**
Hor/Ver/Ang/Bisect/Offset/ < From Point > : **B**
Angle vertex point: Enter the vertex point
Angle start point: Enter a point
Angle end point: Enter a point   *(You could use object snaps to select a point)*
Angle end point: ↵

Offset

The **Offset** option creates Xlines that are parallel to the selected line/Xline at the specified offset distance. The offset distance can be specified by entering a numerical value or picking two points on the screen. If you select the through option, then the offset line will pass through the selected point. (This option works like the OFFSET editing command.)

NURBS- BASED ELLIPSE

Up to release 12, the ellipses were based on polylines. They were made of multiple polyarcs as a result of which it was difficult to edit an ellipse. For example, if you select an ellipse, the grips will be displayed at the end points of each polyarc. If you move a vertex point, you get a shape as shown in Figure 3-5(b). Also, you cannot snap to the center or the quadrant points of a polyline based ellipse. In AutoCAD release 13, you can still draw the polyline-based ellipse by setting the value of **PELLIPSE** system variable to 1. The default value of PELLIPSE is 0, which creates a NURBS (Non Uniform Rational Bezier Splines) ellipse. The NURBS based ellipse has a center and quadrant points. If you select it, the grips will be displayed at the center and the quadrant points of the ellipse. If you move one of the grips located on the perimeter of the ellipse, the major or minor axis will change that results in the change of ellipse size as shown in Figure 3-5(d).

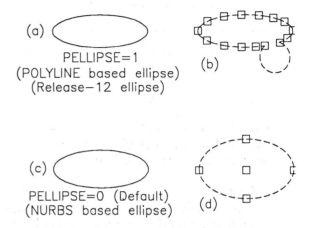

Figure 3-5 Drawing polyline and NURBS based ellipses

Drawing Elliptical Arcs

You can use the Arc option of the NURBS-based ELLIPSE command (PELLIPSE=0) to draw an elliptical arc. When you enter the ELLIPSE command and select the Arc option, AutoCAD will prompt you enter information about the geometry of the ellipse and the arc limits. You can define the arc limits by using the following options

1. Start and End angle of the arc
2. Start and Included angle of the arc
3. Specifying Start and End parameters

The angles are measured with the positive X axis and in counter-clockwise direction, if AutoCAD's default set up has not been changed. The following example illustrates the use of these three options:

Example 1

Draw the following elliptical arcs
      a. Start angle = -45   End angle = 135
      b. Start angle = -45   Included angle = 225
      c. Start parameter = @1,0   End parameter = @1<225

Specifying Start and End Angle of the Arc
Command: **ELLIPSE**
Arc/Center/<Axis endpoint 1>: **A**
Arc/Center/<Axis endpoint 1>: *Select the first endpoint*
Axis endpoint 2: *Select the second endpoint*
<Other axis distance>/Rotation: *Select a point or enter distance*
Parameter/Include/<start angle>: **-45**
Parameter/Include/<end angle>: **135** *(Angle where arc ends)*

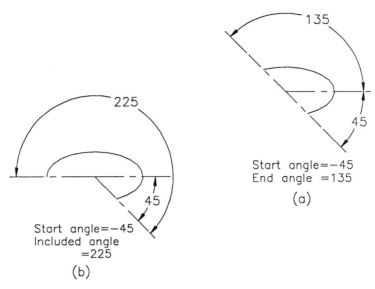

Figure 3-6 Drawing NURBS-based ellipses

Specifying Start and Included Angle of the Arc

Command: **ELLIPSE**
Arc/Center/ < Axis endpoint 1 > : **A**
Arc/Center/ < Axis endpoint 1 > : *Select the first endpoint*
Axis endpoint 2: *Select the second endpoint*
< Other axis distance > /Rotation: *Select a point or enter distance*
Parameter/Include/ < start angle > : **-45**
Parameter/Include/ < end angle > : **225**   *(Included angle)*

Specifying Start and End Parameters

Command: **ELLIPSE**
Arc/Center/ < Axis endpoint 1 > : **A**
Arc/Center/ < Axis endpoint 1 > : *Select the first endpoint*
Axis endpoint 2: *Select the second endpoint*
< Other axis distance > /Rotation: *Select a point or enter distance*
Parameter/Include/ < start angle > : **A**
Angle/ < start parameter > : **@1,0**
Angle/Include/ < end parameter > : **@1<225**

Calculating Parameters for Elliptical Arc

The start and end parameters of an elliptical arc are determined by specifying a point on the circle whose diameter is equal to the major diameter of the ellipse as shown in Figure 3-7. In this drawing, the major axis of the ellipse is 2.0 and the minor axis is 1.0. The diameter of the circle is 2.0. To determine the start and end parameters of the elliptical arc, you must specify the points on the circle. In Example-1, the start parameter is @1,0 and the end parameter is @1,225. Once you specify the points on the circle, AutoCAD will project these points on the major axis and determine the end point of the elliptical arc. In Figure 3-7, Q is the end parameter of the elliptical arc. AutoCAD projects the point Q on the major axis and locates the intersection point P. The point P is the end point of the elliptical arc. The coordinates of the point P can be calculated by using the following equations:

$$\text{The equation of ellipse with center as origin is}$$
$$x^2/a^2 + y^2/b^2 = 1$$

*In parametric form x = a * cos(u)*
*y = b * sin(u)*

For Example 1
a = 1
b = 0.5
Therefore
*x = 1 * cos(225) = -0.707*
*y = 0.5 * sin(225) = -0.353*
The coordinates of point P are (-0.707,- 0.353) with respect to the center of ellipse.

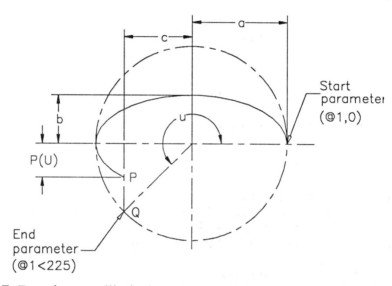

Figure 3-7 Drawing an elliptical arc by specifying the start and end parameters

CREATING NURBS SPLINES

The **NURBS** splines can be created by using **SPLINE** command. NURBS is an acronym for Nonuniform Rational Bezier-Spline. The spline created by SPLINE command is different from the spline created by using PEDIT command. The Non-Uniform aspect of the spline enables the spline to have sharp corners because the spacing between the spline elements that constitute a spline can be irregular. The Rational means that the irregular geometry like arcs, circles, and ellipses can be combined with free form curves. The Bezier-Spline (B-Spline) is the core that enables accurate fitting of curves to input data with Bezier's curve fitting interface. The SPLINE command can be invoked from the pull-down menu (Select Draw/ Spline), screen menu (Select DRAW1/ Spline:), or by entering SPLINE command at AutoCAD's command prompt. The following is the command prompt sequence for creating the spline as shown in Figure 3-8:

Figure 3-8 Selecting SPLINE command from the pull-down menu

Command: **SPLINE**
Object/<Enter first point>: Select point, P1
Enter point: Select the second point, P2
Close/Fit Tolerance/<Enter point>: *Select point, P3*
Close/Fit Tolerance/<Enter point>: *Select point, P4*
Close/Fit Tolerance/<Enter point>: *Select point, P5*
Close/Fit Tolerance/<Enter point>: *Select point, P6*
Close/Fit Tolerance/<Enter point>: ↵
Enter start tangent: ↵ *(Press Enter key for default)*
Enter end tangent: *Select point P7*

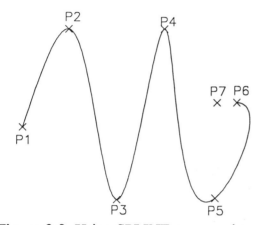

Figure 3-9 Using SPLINE command to draw splines

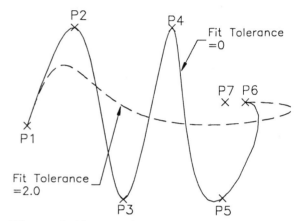

Figure 3-10 Creating a spline with Fit Tolerance of 2

SPLINE Command Options

Object
The Object option allows you to change a 2D or 3D splined polyline into a NURBS spline. The original splined polyline is deleted if the system variable DELOB is set to 0. To change a polyline into splined polyline, use the PEDIT command.

Command: **SPLINE**
Object/<Enter first point>: **O**
Select object: *Select 2D or 3D splined polyline*

Close
The close option allows you to close the NURBS spline. When you use this option, AutoCAD will automatically join the end point with the start point of the spline and you will be prompted to define the start tangent only.

Fit Tolerance
The Fit Tolerance option allows you to control the fit of the spline between the specified points. By entering a smaller value, the spline will pass through the defined points as close as possible, Figure 3-10. If the fit tolerance value is 0, the spline passes through the fit points.

Command: **SPLINE**
Object/<Enter first point>: *Select first point*
Enter point: *Select second point*
Close/Fit Tolerance/<Enter point>: **F**
Enter Fit Tolerance <current>: *Enter a value*
Close/Fit Tolerance/<Enter point>: *Select third point*

Start and End Tangents

The Start and End tangent allows you to control the tangency of the spline at the start and end points of the spline. If you press the Enter key at these prompts, AutoCAD will use the default value. By default, the tangency is determined by the slope of the spline at the specified point.

EDITING SPLINES

(SPLINEDIT Command)

The NURBS splines can be edited by using the **SPLINEDIT** command. With this command you can fit data in the selected spline, close or open the spline, move vertex points, refine, or reverse a spline. The SPLINEDIT command can be invoked from the pull-down menu (Select Modify/ Edit spline), screen menu (Select MODIFY/ Spline Ed:), or by entering **SPLINEDIT** command at AutoCAD's Command prompt. The following is the prompt sequence of SPLINEDIT command:

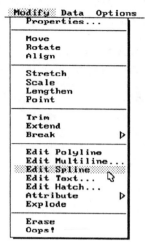

Figure 3-11 Selecting SPLINEDIT command from the pull-down menu

Command: **SPLINEDIT**
Select spline:
Fit Data/Close/Move Vertex/Refine/rEverse/Undo/eXit < X > :

Fit Data

When you draw a spline, the spline is fit to the specified points (data points). The **Fit Data** option allows you to edit these points (fit data points). For example, if you want to redefine the start and end tangents of a spline, select the Fit Data option and then select the Tangents option as follows:

Command: **SPLINEDIT**
Select spline:
Fit Data/Close/Move Vertex/Refine/rEverse/Undo/eXit < X > : **F**
Add/Close/Delete/Move/Purge/Tangents/toLerance/eXit < X > : **T**
System Default/ < Enter start tangent > : *Select a point (P0)*
System Default/ < Enter end tangent > : *Select a point (P7)*

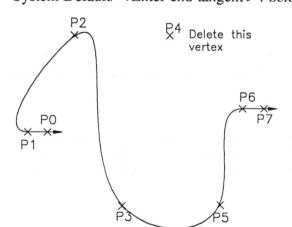

Figure 3-12 Using SPLINEDIT command to fit data points

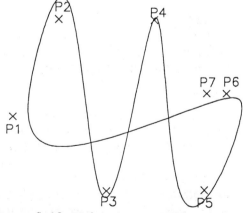

Figure 3-13 Using SPLINEDIT command to close a spline

Close

The **Close** option allows you to close or open a spline. When you select the Close option, AutoCAD lets you open, move the vertex, refine or reverse the spline. The following is the command prompt sequence for closing a polyline, Figure 3-13:

Fit Data/Close/Move Vertex/Refine/rEverse/Undo/eXit<X>: **C**
Open/Move Vertex/Refine/rEverse/Undo/eXit<X>: **X**

Move Vertex

When you draw a spline, it is associated with Bezier Control Frame. The **Move Vertex** option allows you to move the vertices of the control frame. To display the frame with the spline, set the value of SPLFRAME system variable to 1. The following is the command prompt sequence for moving one of the vertex points, Figure 3-14:

Fit Data/Close/Move Vertex/Refine/rEverse/Undo/eXit<X>: **M**
Next/Previous/Select Point/eXit/ <Enter new location>: S
Select point: *Select a point (P1)*
Next/Previous/Select Point/eXit/ <Enter new location>: *Enter new location (P0)*
Next/Previous/Select Point/eXit/ <Enter new location>: **X**

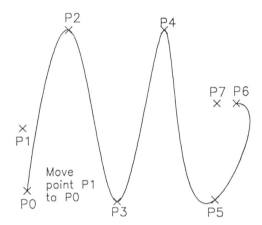

Figure 3-14 Using SPLINEDIT command to move vertex points

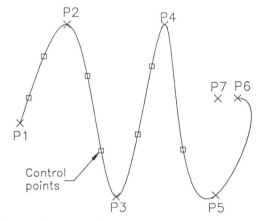

Figure 3-15 Using SPLINEDIT command to refine a spline

Refine

The **Refine** option allows you to refine a spline by adding more control points in the spline, elevating the order, or adding weight to vertex points. For example, if you want to add more control points to a spline, the command prompt sequence is as follows: (Figure 3-14)

Fit Data/Close/Move Vertex/Refine/rEverse/Undo/eXit<X>: **R**
Add control points/Elevate Order/Weight/eXit <X>: **A**
Select a point on the spline: *Select a point*
Select a point on the spline: ◄─┘
Add control points/Elevate Order/Weight/eXit <X>: **X**

Reverse

The **Reverse** option allows you to reverse the spline direction.

Undo

The **Undo** option undoes the previous option.

Exit

The **eXit** option exits the command prompt.

Exercise

First draw the figure as shown at the top and then use the SPLINE, SPLINEDIT, and GRIPS commands to obtain the figure as shown in the bottom drawing (Figure 3-16). (Set the SNAP=0.05. Also, assume the missing dimensions)

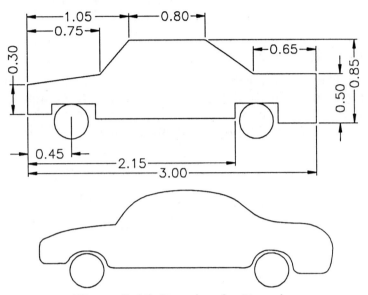

Figure 3-16 Drawing for Exercise

4

Multilines

CREATING MULTILINES

AutoCAD's Multiline feature allows the user to draw composite lines that consists of multiple parallel lines. You can draw these lines by using **MLINE** command. Before drawing the multilines, you need to set the multiline style. This can be accomplished by using **MLSTYLE** command. Also, the editing of the multilines is made possible by **MLEDIT** command.

DEFINING MULTILINE STYLE (MLSTYLE Command)

The **MLSTYLE** command allows you to set the style of multilines. You can specify the number of elements in the multiline and the properties of each element. The style also controls the end caps, end lines, and the background color of multilines. When you enter this command, AutoCAD displays the **Multiline Styles** dialogue box on the screen. Through this dialogue box, you can set the spacing between the parallel lines, linetype pattern, colors, solid background fill, and the capping arrangements. By default, the multiline style (STANDARD) has two lines that are offset at 0.5 and -0.5.

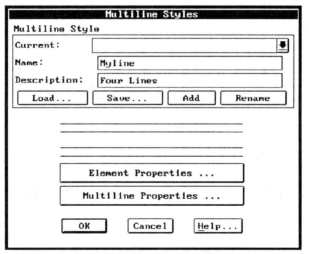

Figure 4-1 Multiline Style dialogue box

The Multiline Style has the following options:

Current:
The **Current** edit box displays and sets the current multiline style. If several styles have been defined, the name of the current style is displayed in the current edit box. You can use the arrow button to pop up the list of the predefined styles and make any style current. The list of multiline styles can include the multiline styles that have been defined in an externally referenced drawing (Xref drawings).

Name:
The **Name** edit box lets you enter the name of the multiline style that you are defining. You can also use it to rename a style.

Description:
The **Description** edit box allows you to enter the description of the multiline style. The length of the description can be up to 255 characters, including spaces.

Load...
The **Load...** button allows you to load a multiline style from an external multiline library file (acad.mln). When you select this button, AutoCAD displays the **Load Multiline Style dialogue box**. From this dialogue box you can select the style that you want to make current. You can also use this dialogue box to load a predefined multiline file (.mln file) by selecting the **File...** button and then selecting the file that you want to load. Once the file is loaded, you can select a style that is defined in the **.mln** file.

Save...
The **Save...** button lets you save or copy the current multiline style to an external file (.mln file). When you select this button, AutoCAD displays the **Save multiline styles** dialogue box listing the names of the predefined multiline style (.mln) files. From the file listing, select the file or enter the name of the file where you want to save the current multiline style.

Add
The **Add** button allows you to add the multiline style name (Style name displayed in the Name edit box) to the current multiline file (.mln file).

Rename
The **Rename** button allows you to rename the current multiline style. It will rename the multiline style that is displayed in the Current: edit box to the name that is displayed in the Name: edit box. You cannot rename the **Standard** multiline style.

Line Display Panel
The **Multiline Styles** dialogue box also displays the multiline configuration in the display panel. The panel will display the color, linetype, and the relative spacing of the lines.

Element Properties

From the **Multiline Styles** dialogue box, if you select the Element Properties... button, AutoCAD will display the **Element Properties** dialogue box. This dialogue box provides you the following options for setting the properties of individual lines (elements) that constitute the multiline.

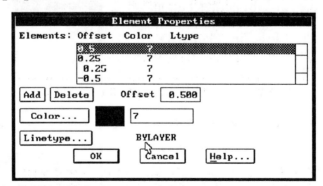

Figure 4-2 Element Properties dialogue box

Elements
The **Elements** box displays the offset, color, and linetype of each line that constitutes the current multiline style. The lines are always listed in descending order based on the offset distance. For example, a line with 0.5 offset will be listed first and a line with 0.25 offset will be listed next.

Add

The Add button lets you add new lines to the current line style. The maximum number of lines that you can add is sixteen. When you select the Add button, AutoCAD inserts a line with the offset distance of 0.00. After the line is added, you can change its offset distance, color, or linetype by selecting Offset, Color..., or Linetype... buttons.

Delete

The **Delete** button allows you to delete the line that is highlighted in the Elements list box.

Offset

The **Offset** button allows you to change the offset distance of the selected line in the Elements list box. The offset distance is defined with respect to the origin 0,0. The offset distance can be a positive or a negative value, that enables you to center the lines.

Color...

The **Color...** button allows you to assign a color to the selected line. When you select this button, AutoCAD displays the standard color dialogue box (Select Color dialogue box). You can select a color from the dialogue box or by entering a color number or name in the edit box that is located to the right of the color swatch box in the Element Properties dialogue box.

Linetype...

The **Linetype...** button allows you to assign a linetype to the selected line. When you select this button, AutoCAD displays the standard linetype dialogue box (Select Linetypes dialogue box). After selecting the linetype, pick the OK button to exit the dialogue box.

Note
When you make changes in the element properties or the multiline properties, the current multiline style may not get updated. To resolve such problems, add the multiline style to the current multiline style (.mln) file. This can be accomplished by entering the new style name in the Name: edit box of Multiline Styles dialogue box and then selecting the Add button.

Multiline Properties

If you select the Multiline Line properties button from the "Multiline Style" dialogue box, AutoCAD will display the **Multiline Properties** dialogue box. You can use this dialogue box to define Multiline properties like display joints, end caps, and the background fill. The dialogue box provides the following options:

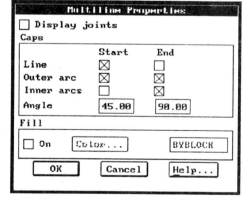

Display Joints

If you select the Display joints check box, AutoCAD will display a **miter** line across all elements of the multiline at the point where two multilines meet. If you draw only one multiline segment, no miter line is drawn because there is no intersection point.

Figure 4-3 Multiline Properties dialogue box

Line

The **Line** option draws a line cap at the start and end of each multiline. It has two check boxes that control the start and end caps.

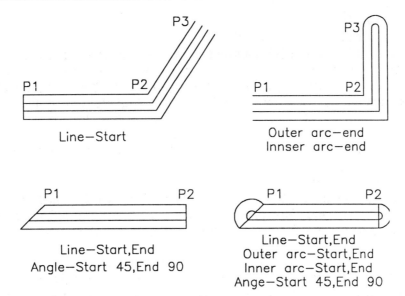

Figure 4-4 Drawing multilines with different end cap specifications

Outer Arc

The **Outer arc** option draws an arc (semicircle) between the end points of the outermost lines.

Inner Arc

The **Inner arc** options control the inner arcs at the start and end of a multiline. The arc is drawn between the even numbered inner lines. For example, if there are two inner lines, an arc will be drawn at the ends of these lines. However, if there are three inner lines, the middle line is not capped with an arc.

Angle

The **Angle** option controls the cap angle at the start and end of a multiline. The value of this angle can be from 10 degrees to 170 degrees.

Fill

The **Fill** option toggles the background fill on and off. If the fill is On, you can select the color of the background fill by selecting the color button. When you select this button, AutoCAD will display the standard color dialogue box. The color can also be set by entering the color name or color number in the edit box located to the right of color swatch box.

DRAWING MULTILINES (MLINE Command)

The **MLINE** command can be used to draw multilines. It can be invoked from the screen menu (Select DRAW 1/ Mline:) or pull-down menu (Select Draw/ Multiline). The command can also be invoked by entering **MLINE** command at AutoCAD's command prompt. The following is the command prompt sequence of **MLINE** command:

Command: **MLINE**
Justification=Top, Scale=1.00, Style=Mystyle1
Justification/Scale/STyle/ <From point>: *Select a point*
To point: *Select the second point*
Undo/ <To point>: *Select next point or enter U for undo*
Close/Undo/ <To point>: *Select next point, enter U, or C for close*

When you enter the **MLINE** command, it always displays the status of the multiline justification, scale, and style name. The command provides the following options:

Justification Option

The justification determines how a multiline is drawn between the specified points. Three justifications are available for MLINE command, Top, Zero, and Bottom.

Top

The **Top** justification produces a multiline so that the top line coincides with the selected points. Since the line offsets in a multiline is arranged in descending order, the line with the largest positive offset will coincide with the selected points.

Zero

The **Zero** option will produce a multiline so that the zero offset position of the multiline coincides with the selected points. In other words, the multilines will be centered if the positive and negative offsets are equal.

Bottom

The **Bottom** option will produce a multiline in which the bottom line, line with least offset distance, coincides with the selected point when the line is drawn from left to right.

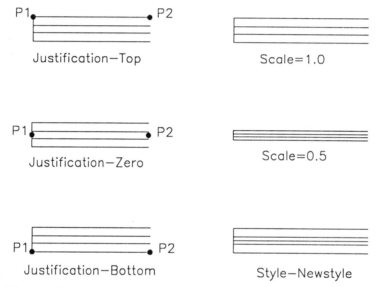

Figure 4-5 Drawing multilines with different justifications

Scale Option

The **Scale** option allows you to change the scale of the multiline. For example, if the scale factor is 0.5 the distance between the lines (offset distance) will be reduced to half. Therefore the width of the multiline will be half of what was defined in the multiline style. A negative scale factor will flip the order of the offset lines. Multilines are drawn so that the line with maximum offset distance is at the top and the line with the least offset distance is at the bottom. If you enter a scale factor of -0.5, the order in which the lines are drawn will get flipped and the offset distances will get reduced by half. (The line with the least offset will be drawn at the top.). Here it is assumed that the lines are drawn from left to right. If the lines are drawn from right to left, the offsets are reversed. Also, if the scale factor is 0, AutoCAD forces the multiline into a single line. The line still possesses the properties of a multiline. The scale does not effect the linetype scale (LTSCALE).

STyle Option

The **Style** option allows you to change the current multiline style. The style must be predefined before using the STyle option to change the style.

EDITING MULTILINES

(Using GRIPS)

The multilines can be edited by using grips. When you select a multiline the grips appear at the end points based on the justification used when drawing multilines. For example, if the multilines are top justified then the grips will be displayed at the end point of the first (top) line segment. Similarly, for zero and bottom justified multilines the grips are displayed on the center and bottom line respectively.

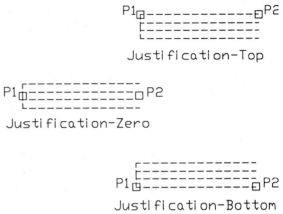

Figure 4-6 Using GRIPS to edit multilines

Note

Multilines do not support some of the editing commands like BREAK, CHAMFER, FILLET, TRIM or EXTEND. However, commands like COPY, MOVE, MIRROR, STRETCH, EXPLODE and some Object Snap modes can be used with multilines. You must use MLEDIT command to edit multilines. MLEDIT command has several options that makes it easier to edit these lines.

EDITING MULTILINES

(Using MLEDIT Command)

The **MLEDIT** command can be invoked from the screen menu (Select MODIFY/ Mledit:), pull-down menu (Select Modify/ Mledit...), or by entering MLEDIT command at AutoCAD's Command: prompt.

Command: **MLEDIT**

When you enter this command, AutoCAD will display the **Multiline Edit Tools** dialogue box on the screen. The dialogue box contains five basic editing tools. To edit a multiline, first select the editing operation that you want to perform by double clicking on the image tile or by picking the image tile and then picking the OK button. Once you have selected the editing option, AutoCAD will prompt you to select the object or select the points, depending on the option you have selected. After you are done editing, if you press the Enter key the dialogue box will return and you can continue editing. The following is the list of options for editing multilines.

Intersection - Cross
    Closed Cross
    Open Cross
    Merged Cross
Intersection - Tee
    Closed Tee
    Open Tee
    Merged Tee
Corner Joint
Vertices - Adding/Deleting
    Add Vertex
    Delete Vertex
Lines - Cutting/Welding

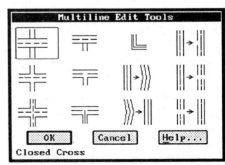

Figure 4-7 Multiline Edit Tools dialogue box

Cut Single
Cut All
Weld

Intersections - Cross

Using the **MLEDIT** command options you can create three types of cross intersections, Closed, Open, and Merged. You must be careful how you select the objects, because the order in which you select the objects determines the edited shape of a multiline, Figure 4-8. The multilines can belong to the same multiline or two completely different multilines. The following is the command prompt sequence for creating Intersection-Cross

Command: **MLEDIT**
Select first mline: *Select the first multiline*
Select second mline: *Select the second multiline*
Select first mline (or Undo):

If you select undo, AutoCAD undoes the operation and prompts you to select the first mline. However, if you select another multiline, AutoCAD will prompt you to select the second multiline. If you press the Enter key twice, the "Multiline Edit Tools" dialogue box is returned.

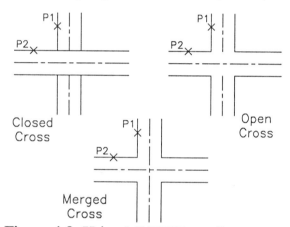

Figure 4-8 Using MLEDIT to edit multilines (Intersection Cross)

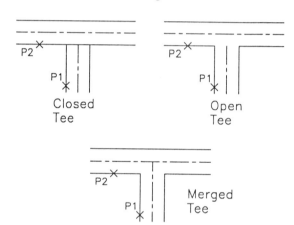

Figure 4-9 Using MLEDIT to edit multilines (Intersection Tee)

Intersections - Tee

Using **MLEDIT** command options you can create three types of tee shaped intersections, Closed, Open, and Merged. Like intersection cross, you must be careful how you select the objects, because the order in which you select the objects determines the edited shape of a multiline, Figure 4-9. The prompt sequence for Intersections-Tee is same as Intersections-Cross.

Command: **MLEDIT**
Select first mline: *Select the first multiline*
Select second mline: *Select the intersecting multiline*
Select first mline (or Undo): *Select another multiline, enter Undo, or press Enter key*

Corner Joint

The **Corner Joint** option creates a corner joint between the two selected multilines. The multilines must be two separate objects (multilines). When you specify the two multilines, AutoCAD trims or extends the first multiline to intersect with the second multiline. The following is the command prompt sequence for creating a corner joint:

Command: **MLEDIT**
Select first mline: *Select the multiline to trim or extend*
Select second mline: *Select the intersecting multiline*
Select first mline (or Undo): *Select another multiline, enter Undo, or press Enter key*

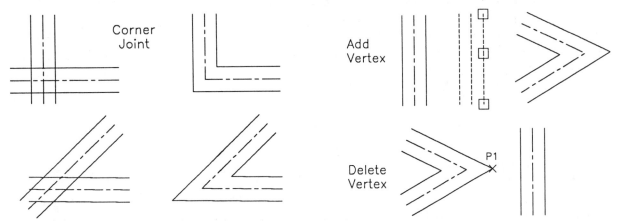

Figure 4-10 Using MLEDIT to edit multilines (Corner Joint)

Figure 4-11 Using MLEDIT to edit multilines (Adding or deleting vertices)

Vertices - Adding/Deleting

You can use the **MLEDIT** command to add or delete the vertices of a multiline. When you select a multiline for adding a vertex, AutoCAD inserts a vertex point at the point where the object was selected. If you want to move the vertex, use GRIPS. Similarly, you can use **MLEDIT** command to delete the vertices by selecting the object whose vertex point you want to delete. AutoCAD removes the vertex that is in the positive direction of the selected multiline segment.

Command: **MLEDIT**
Select mline: *Select the multiline for adding vertex*
Select mline (or Undo): *Select another multiline, enter undo, or press Enter key*

Lines - Cutting/Welding

You can use the **MLEDIT** command for cutting or welding the lines. When you cut a multiline, it does not create two separate multilines. They are still a part of the same object (multiline). Also, the points selected for cutting the multiline do not have to be on the same element of the multiline, Figure 4-12.

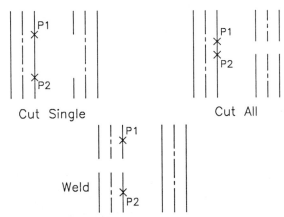

Figure 4-12 Using MLEDIT to edit multilines (Lines, Cutting/Welding)

Command: **MLEDIT**
Select mline: *Select the multiline. The point where you select the multiline specifies the first cut point*
Select second point: *Select the second cut point*
Select mline (or Undo): *Select another multiline, enter Undo, or press Enter key*

The weld option welds the multilines that have been cut by using MLEDIT command options, Figure 4-12.

Command: **MLEDIT**
Select mline: *Select the multiline.*
Select second point: *Select the second multiline*
Select mline (or Undo): *Select another multiline, enter Undo, or press Enter key*

COMMAND LINE INTERFACE FOR MLEDIT COMMAND

You can also edit the multilines without using the "Multiline Edit Tools" dialogue box. To accomplish this, enter **-MLEDIT** command at AutoCAD's Command: prompt.

Command: **-MLEDIT**
Mline editing options AV/DV/CC/OC/MC/CT/OT/MT/CJ/CS/CA/WA:

After selecting an option, AutoCAD will prompt you to select the multilines or specify points. The prompt sequence will depend on the option you select as discussed earlier under MLEDIT command. The following is the description of the command line options:

AV	Add Vertex		OT	Open Tee
DV	Delete Vertex		MT	Merged Tee
CC	Closed Cross		CJ	Corner Joint
OC	Open Cross		CS	Cut Single
MC	Merged Cross		CA	Cut All
CT	Closed Tee		WA	Weld All

SYSTEM VARIABLES FOR MLINE

CMLJUST	Store the justification of the current multiline
CMLSCALE	Stores the scale of the current multiline
CMLSTYLE	Stores the name of the current multiline style

Example 1

In the following example you will create a Multiline Style that represents a wood framed wall system. The wall system consists of 1/2" wallboard, 3 1/2" 2x4 in. wood stud, and 1/2" wallboard.

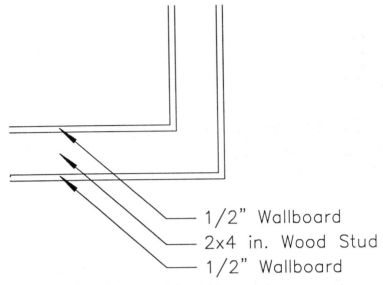

1/2" Wallboard
2x4 in. Wood Stud
1/2" Wallboard

Figure 4-13 Creating a multistyle for wood frame wall system

Step 1
Use the **MLSTYLE** command to display the Multiline Styles dialogue box. The current style STANDARD will be edited to create the new multiline style.

Step 2
Select the **Name** edit box and replace the word **STANDARD** with **2x4_Wood**.

Step 3
Select the **Description** edit box and enter **Wallboard Wood Framed 2x4 Partition**.

Step 4
Select the **Element Properties...** button to display the Element Properties dialogue box. The Element properties of the STANDARD multiline style remain.

Step 5
Select the **0.5** line definition in the **Elements** display box. Select the **Offset** edit box and replace **0.500** with **1.75**. This redefines the first line as being 1.75" above the center line of the wall.

Step 6
Select the **-0.5** line definition in the **Elements** display box. Select the **Offset** edit box and replace **0.500** with **-1.75**. This redefines the second line as being 1.75" below the center line of the wall.

Step 7
Select the **Add** button to add a new line to the current line style.

Step 8
Select the new **0.0** line definition in the **Elements** display box. Select the **Offset** edit box and replace **0.000** with **2.25**.

Step 9

Select the **Color** edit box and replace **BYLAYER** with **YELLOW**.

Step 10

Repeat steps 7 to 9 this time using the value -2.25 in step 8 to add another line to the current line style.

Step 11

Select the **OK** button to accept the changes to the **Element Properties** and return to the **Multiline Styles** dialogue box. The new multiline style will be displayed.

Step 12

Select the **Add** button to add the new style to the current multiline file.

Step 13

Select the **Save...** button to save the current multiline style to an external file for use in later drawing sessions. From the file listing, select the file or enter the name of the file where you want to save the current multiline style.

Step 14

Select the **OK** button to return to the drawing editor. To test the new multiline style use the **MLINE** command and draw a series of lines.

Complex Linetypes
Current Linetype Scaling
5 Modifying Associative Hatch

COMPLEX LINETYPES

AutoCAD has provided a facility to create complex linetypes. The complex linetypes can be classified into two groups; String Complex Linetype and Shape Complex Linetype. The difference between the two is that the String Complex Linetype has a text string inserted in the line, whereas the Shape Complex Linetype has a shape inserted in the line. The facility of creating complex linetypes increases the functionality of lines. For example, if you want to draw a line around the building that indicates the fence line, you can do it by defining a Complex Linetype that will automatically give you the desired line with the text string (Fence). Similarly, you can define Complex Linetype that will insert a shape (symbols) at predefined distances along the line.

CREATING A STRING COMPLEX LINETYPES

When writing the definition of a String Complex Linetype, the actual text and its attributes must be included in the linetype definition. The format of the String Complex Linetype is:

["String", Text Style, Text Height, Rotation, X-Offset, Y-Offset]

The following are the attributes and their description that must be assigned to the text string:

String
It is the actual text that you want to insert along the line. The text string must be enclosed in quotation marks (").

Text style
It is the name of the text style file that you want to use for generating the text string. The text style must be predefined.

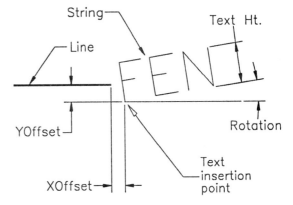

Figure 5-1 The attributes of a String Complex Linetype

Rotation
It is the rotation of the text string with respect to the positive X axis, if AutoCAD is configured to measure angles with the positive X axis.

Text Height
It is the actual height of the text. In Figure 5-1 the height of the text is 0.1 units.

35

X-Offset

It is the distance of the lower left corner of the text string from the end point of the line segment measured along the line. If the line is horizontal, then X-Offset distance is measured along the X axis. In Figure 5-1(a), the X-Offset distance is 0.05.

Y-Offset

It is the distance of the lower left corner of the text string from the end point of the line segment measured perpendicular to the line. If the line is horizontal, then the Y-Offset distance is measured along the Y axis. In Figure 5-1(a), the Y-Offset distance is -0.05. The distance is minus because the start point of the text string is 0.05 units below the end point of the first line segment.

Example 1

In the following example you will write the definition of a String Complex Linetype that consists of the text string "Fence" and line segments. The length of the line segments is 0.75. The height of the text string is 0.1 units and the space between the end of the text string and the following line segment is 0.05.

Step 1

Before writing the definition of a new linetype, it is important to determine the line specification. One of the ways it can be done is to actually draw the lines and the text the way you want it to appear in the drawing. Once you have drawn the line and the text to your satisfaction, measure the distances that are needed to define the String Complex Linetype. In this example the values are given as follows:

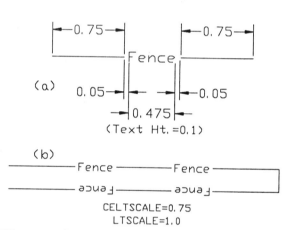

Figure 5-2 The attributes of the String Complex Linetype and line specifications for Example 1

Text string	Fence
Text style	Standard
Text height	0.1
Text rotation	0
X-Offset	0.05
Y-Offset	-0.05

Length of the first line segment = 0.75
Distance between the line segments = 0.575

Step 2

Use a text editor to write the definition of the String Complex Linetype. You can add the definition to AutoCAD's ACAD.LIN file or create a separate file. The extension of the file must be .LIN. The following file is the listing of the FENCE.LIN file for Example 1. The name of the linetype is NEWFence.

```
*NEWFence,New fence boundary line
A,0.75,["Fence",Standard,S=0.1,A=0,X=0.05,Y=-0.05],-0.575
```

Step 3

To test the linetype, load the linetype using **LINETYPE** command with Load option and assign it to a layer. Draw a line or any object to check if the line is drawn to the given specifications. Notice that the text is drawn upside down when you draw a line from right to left. When you draw a polyline, circle, or spline, the text string does not align with the object.

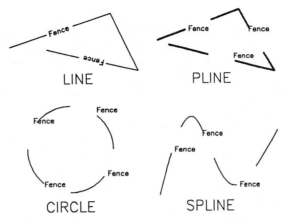

Figure 5-3 Using String Complex Linetype

Step 4

In the NEWFence linetype definition the specified angle is 0 degrees, (Absolute angle A=0). Therefore, when you use the NEWFence linetype to draw a circle, polyline, or a spline, the text string (Fence) will be at zero degrees. If you want the text string (Fence) to align with the polyline, spline, or circle, specify the angle as relative angle (R=0) in the NEWFence linetype definition. The following is the linetype definition for NEWFence linetype with relative angle R=0.

*NEWFence,New fence boundary line
A,0.75,["Fence",Standard,S=0.1,R=0,X=0.05,Y=-0.05],-0.575

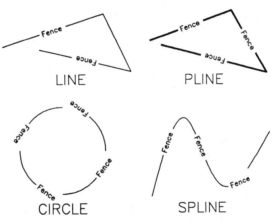

Figure 5-4 Using String Complex Linetype with angle (R=0)

Step 5

In Figure 5-4, you might have noticed that the text string is not properly aligned with the circumference of the circle. This is because AutoCAD draws the text string in a direction that is tangent to the circle at the text insertion point. To resolve this problem you must define the middle point of the text string as the insertion point. Also, the line specifications should be measured accordingly. The following figure, Figure 5-5, gives the measurements of the NEWFence linetype with middle point of the text as insertion point.

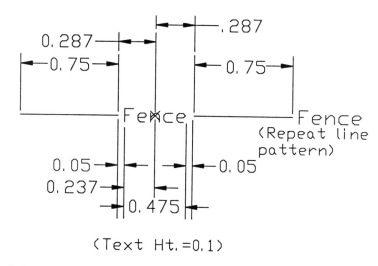

(Text Ht.=0.1)

Figure 5-5 Specifications of String Complex Linetype with the middle point of the text string as the text insertion point

The following is the linetype definition for NEWFence linetype.

```
*NEWFence,New fence boundary line
A,0.75,-0.287,["FENCE",Standard,S=0.1,X=-0.237,Y=-0.05],-0.287
```

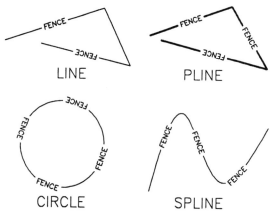

Figure 5-6 Using String Complex Linetype with the middle point of the text string as the text insertion point

Note

If no angle is defined in the line definition, it defaults to angle R=0.

CREATING A SHAPE COMPLEX LINETYPES

Like the String Complex Linetype, when you write the definition of a Shape Complex Linetype, the name of the shape, name of the shape file, and other shape attribute like rotation, scale, X-Offset, and Y-Offset must be included in the linetype definition. The format of the Shape Complex Linetype is:

[Shape Name, Shape File, Scale, Rotation, X-Offset, Y-Offset]

The following are the attributes and their description that must be assigned to the shape:

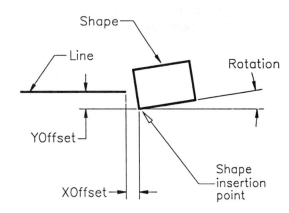

Shape Name

It is the name of the shape that you want to insert along the line. The shape name must exist, otherwise no shape will be generated along the line.

Shape File

It is the name of the **compiled** shape file (.SHX) that contains the definition of the shape that is being inserted in the line. The name of the subdirectory where the shape file is located must be in the ACAD search path. The shape files (.SHP) must be compiled before using the SHAPE command to load the shape.

Figure 5-7 The attributes of a Shape Complex Linetype

Scale

It is the scale of the inserted shape. If the scale is 1, the size of the shape will be same as defined in the shape definition (.SHP file).

Rotation

It is the rotation of the shape with respect to positive X axis, if AutoCAD is configured to measure angles with the positive X axis.

X-Offset

It is the distance of the shape insertion point from the end point of the line segment measured along the line. If the line is horizontal, then X-Offset distance is measured along the X axis. In Figure 5-7 (a), the X-Offset distance is 0.2.

Y-Offset

It is the distance of the shape insertion point from the end point of the line segment measured perpendicular to the line. If the line is horizontal, then the Y-Offset distance is measured along the Y axis. In Figure 5-7(a), the Y-Offset distance is 0.

Example 2

In the following example you will write the definition of a Shape Complex Linetype that consists of the shape (Manhole, the name of the shape is MH) and a line. The length of each line segment is 0.75 and, the scale of the shape is 0.1. The space between the line segments is 0.2.

Step 1

Before writing the definition of a new linetype, it is important to determine the line specifications. One of the ways it can be done is to actually draw the lines and the shape the way you want it to appear in the drawing. Once you have drawn the line and the shape to your satisfaction, measure the distances that are needed to define the Shape Complex Linetype. In this example the values are given as follows:

Shape name	MH
Shape file name	MHOLE.SHX (Name of the compiled shape file)
Scale	0.1
Rotation	0
X-Offset	0.2
Y-Offset	0

Length of the first line segment = 0.75
Distance between the line segments = 0.2

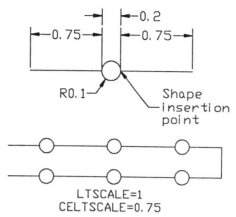

Figure 5-8 The attributes of the Shape Complex Linetype and line specifications for Example 2

Step 2

Use a text editor to write the definition of the shape file. The extension of the file must be .SHP. The following file is the listing of the MHOLE.SHP file for Example 1. The name of the shape is MH. (For details see the chapter on Shapes and Text Fonts.)

```
*215,9,MH
001,10,(1,007),
001,10,(1,071),0
```

Step 3

Use the COMPILE command to compile the shape file (.SHP file). When you use this command, AutoCAD will prompt you to enter the name of the shape file. For this example, the name is MHOLE.SHP. The following is the command prompt sequence for compiling the shape file:

Command: **COMPILE**
Enter NAME of shape file: **MHOLE**

Step 4

Use a text editor to write the definition of the Shape Complex linetype. You can add the definition to AutoCAD's ACAD.LIN file or create a separate file. The extension of the file must be .LIN. The following file is the listing of the MHOLE.LIN file for Example 1. The name of the linetype is MHOLE.

```
*MHOLE,Line with Manholes
A,0.75,[MH,MHOLE.SHX,S=0.10,X=0.2,Y=0],-0.2
```

Step 5

To test the linetype, load the linetype using **LINETYPE** command with Load option and assign it to a layer. Draw a line or any object to check if the line is drawn to the given specifications. The shape is drawn upside down when you draw a line from right to left.

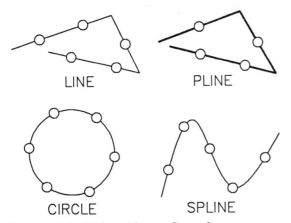

Figure 5-9 Using Shape Complex Linetype

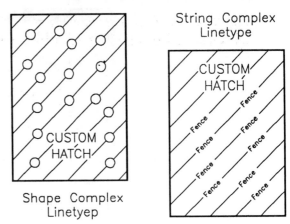

Figure 5-10 Using Shape and String Complex Linetypes to create custom hatch

CURRENT LINETYPE SCALING (CELTSCALE)

Like LTSCALE, the CELTSCALE system variable controls the linetype scaling. The difference is that CELTSCALE determines the current linetype scaling. For example, if you set the CELTSCALE to 0.5, all lines drawn after setting the new value for CELTSCALE will have the linetype scaling factor of 0.5. The value is retained in the CELTSCLAE system variable. The fist line (a) in Figure 5-11 is drawn with the CELTSCALE factor of 1 and the second line (b) is drawn with the CELTSCALE factor of 0.5. The length of the dashed is reduced by a factor of 0.5 when the CELTSCALE is 0.5.

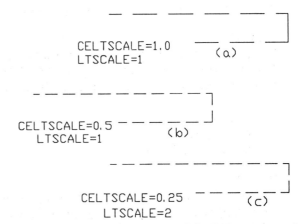

Figure 5-11 Using CELTSCALE to control current linetype scaling

The LTSCALE system variable controls the global scale factor. For example, if LTSCALE is set to 2, all lines in the drawing will be effected by a factor of 2. The net scale factor is equal to the product of CELTSCALE and LTSCALE. Figure 5-11 (c) shows a line that is drawn with LTSCALE of 2 and CELTSCLAE of 0.25. The net scale factor is = LTSCALE x CELTSCLAE = 2 x 0.25 = 0.5

MODIFYING ASSOCIATIVE HATCH

One of the major advantages with the associative hatch feature is that you can edit the hatch pattern or edit the geometry that is hatched. After editing, AutoCAD will automatically regenerate the hatch and the hatch geometry to reflect the changes. The hatch pattern can be edited by using HATCHEDIT command and the hatch geometry can be edited by using GRIPS or some AutoCAD editing commands.

Editing Associative Hatch Pattern (HATCHEDIT Command)

The **HATCHEDIT** command can be used to edit the hatch pattern. When you enter this command, the Hatchedit dialogue box is displayed on the screen.

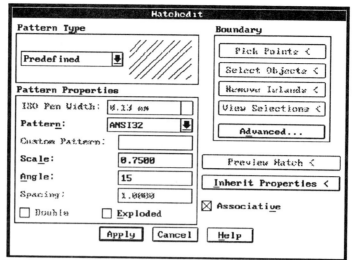

Figure 5-12 Using Hatchedit dialogue box to edit the hatch pattern

You can redefine the hatch pattern by entering the new hatch pattern name in the Pattern edit box. You can also change the scale or angle by entering the new value in the Scale and Angle edit boxes. If you select the Explode button, AutoCAD will remove the associativity of hatch. You can also define the hatch style by picking the Advanced... button and then selecting Normal, Outer, Ignore styles. If you want to copy the properties from an existing hatch pattern, select the Inherit Properties button and then select the hatch. The following figures Figure 5-12 show the hatch patterns before and after editing the hatch pattern.

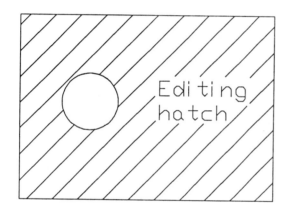

Figure 5-13 ANSI31 hatch pattern

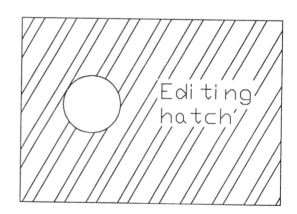

Figure 5-14 Using HATCHEDIT command to edit the hatch pattern

You can also edit the hatch pattern from the Command: prompt line by preceding the BHATCH command with a dash (-). The following is the command prompt sequence for -BHATCH command:

Command: **-BHATCH**
Properties/Select/Remove islands/Advanced/ < internal point > : **P**
Pattern (? or name/U, style): *Enter the pattern name*
Angle for crosshatch lines <0> : *Enter angle*
Spacing between lines <1.00> : *Enter scale*
Double hatch area? <N> : *Enter Y or N*
Properties/Select/Remove islands/Advanced/ < internal point > : **A**
Boundary set/Retain polyline/Island detection/Associativity/ < eXit > : ↵
Properties/Select/Remove islands/Advanced/ < internal point > :

Editing Hatch Boundary

Using GRIPS

One of the ways you can edit the hatch boundary is by using grips. You can select the hatch pattern or the hatch boundaries. If you select the hatch pattern, the hatch highlights and object grips are displayed at the vertex point of each object that defines the boundary of the hatch pattern. If there are any islands or text, the object grips will be displayed at their vertex points. However, if you select an object that defines the hatch boundary, the object grips are displayed at the vertex points of the selected object. Once you change the boundary definition, AutoCAD will re-evaluate the hatch boundary and then hatch the area. When you edit the hatch boundary, make sure that there

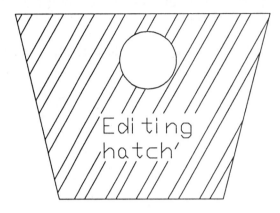

Figure 5-15 Using Object Grips to edit the hatch boundary

are no open spaces in the hatch boundary. AutoCAD **may not** create a hatch if the outer boundary is not closed. Figure 5-15 shows the hatch after moving the circle and text and shortening the bottom edge of the hatch boundary. The entities were edited by using grips.

Using AutoCAD's Editing Commands

When you use the editing commands like MOVE, COPY, SCALE, STRETCH, or MIRROR, the associativity is maintained provided all entities that define the boundary are selected for editing. If any object is missing, the associativity will be lost and AutoCAD will display the following message:

Associativity was removed from (n) hatch block(s)

When you rotate or scale an associative hatch, the new rotation angle and the scale factor is saved with the hatch block's extended object data. This data is then used to update the hatch. If you explode an associative hatch pattern, the associativity between the hatch pattern and the defining boundary is removed. Also, the hatch block is exploded and each line in the hatch pattern becomes a separate object.

Exercise 1

a. Write the definition of a String Complex Linetype (Hot water line) as shown in the following Figure 5-16(a).

a. Write the definition of a String Complex Linetype (Gas line) as shown in the following Figure 5-16(b).

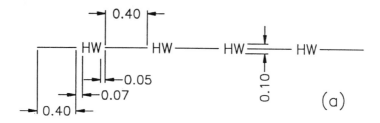

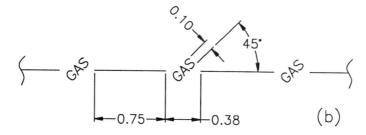

Figure 5-16 Specifications for String Complex Linetype

Exercise 2

Write the shape file for the shape shown in Figure 5-17(a). Compile the shape and use it in defining the Shape Complex linetype so that you can draw a fence line as shown in Figure 5-17(b).

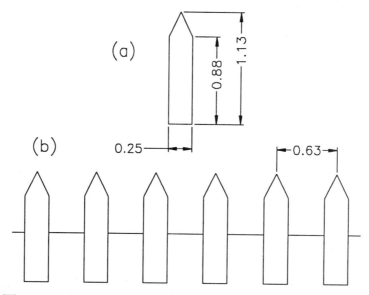

Figure 5-17 Specifications for Shape Complex Linetype

6 Creating Paragraph Text External References

CREATING PARAGRAPH TEXT FOR DOS
(MTEXT Command)

You can use MTEXT command to write a paragraph text whose width can be specified by defining two corners of the text boundary, or by entering the width of the paragraph. The text created by the MTEXT command is a single object regardless of the number of lines it contains. The text boundary is not plotted although it is a part of MTEXT object. The MTEXT command can be invoked from the screen menu (Select DRAW 2/ Mtext:), pull-down menu (Select Draw/ Text/ Text), or by entering MTEXT at AutoCAD's Command: prompt. The following is the command prompt sequence of MTEXT command:

Command: **MTEXT**
Attach/Rotation/Style/Height/Direction/ < Insertion Point > : *Select text insertion point*
Attach/Rotation/Style/Height/Direction/Width/2Points/ < Other corner > : *Select an option or select a point to specify other corner*

Once you are done defining the width of the paragraph text, AutoCAD will automatically assign a files name like ACA00512 and switch to DOS editor where you can enter the text. After you are done entering the text, save the file with the default file name.

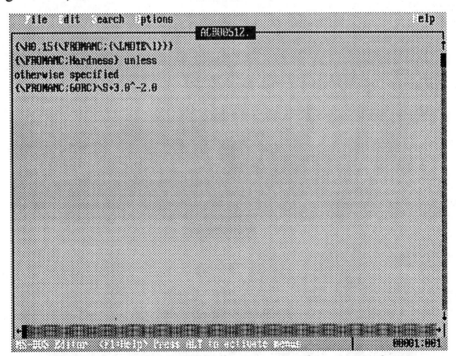

Figure 6-1 Using DOS Editor to enter the paragraph text

MTEXT COMMAND OPTIONS

The MTEXT command has the following options:

Insertion Point

The Insertion Point determines the point where the text will be inserted. For example, if the text justification is top-right (TR), the text paragraph will be to the left and bottom of the insertion point. Similarly, if the text justification is middle-center (MC), the text paragraph will centered around the insertion point, regardless of how you define the width of the paragraph. The insertion point also indicates the first corner of the text boundary.

Other Corner

The point you enter or select at this prompt specifies the other corner of the text boundary. When you define the text boundary, it does not mean that the text paragraph will fit within the defined boundary. AutoCAD only uses the width of the defined boundary as the width of the text paragraph. The height of the text boundary has no effect on the text paragraph. Once you select the other corner, on DOS systems, AutoCAD displays the text editor and automatically assign a file name like AC000512, ACA00512, etc. You can enter the text and once you are done entering the text, save the file. The text will be automatically inserted at the specified insertion point.

Command: **MTEXT**
Attach/Rotation/Style/Height/Direction/ < Insertion Point > : *Select text insertion point*
Attach/Rotation/Style/Height/Direction/Width/2Points/ < Other corner > : **@1.25,0** *(Select an option or select a point to specify other corner)*

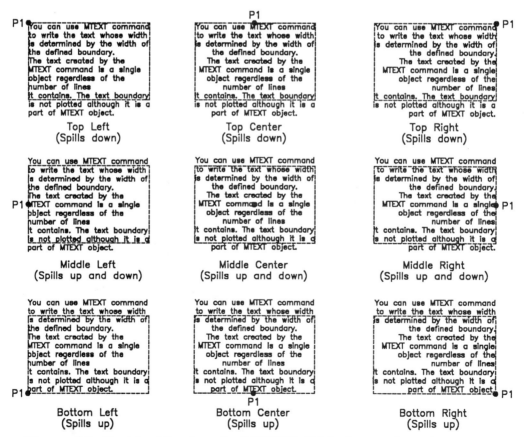

Figure 6-2 Text justifications for MTEXT. P1 is the text insertion point.

Attach

The **Attach** option is used to control the justification of text paragraph. For example, if the text justification is bottom-right (BR), the text paragraph will spill to the left and above the insertion point, regardless of how you define the width of the paragraph.

Command: **MTEXT**
Attach/Rotation/Style/Height/Direction/ < Insertion Point > : **A**
TL/TC/TR/ML/MC/MR/BL/BC/BR: *Select an option*

The drawing of Figure 6-2 shows different text justification for MTEXT.

Rotation

The rotation option specifies the rotation of the text. For example, if the rotation angle is 10 degrees, the text will be rotated 10 degrees in counterclockwise direction.

Style

The **Style** option specifies the text style. The text style that you want to use must be predefined.

Height

The **Height** option specifies the height of the text. Once you specify the height, AutoCAD retains that value unless it is changed. The MTEXT height does not effect the size (TEXTSIZE system variable) specified for TEXT or DTEXT commands.

Direction

The Direction option specifies the direction of the text paragraph. It has two options H for horizontal and V for vertical. In English language the text is read horizontally, therefore entering H or V will not have any effect on the text. However, some languages like Chinese and Japanese, sometimes the text is read vertically.

Width

The **Width** option specifies the width of the text paragraph. The width can be entered by specifying a value or entering a point. The distance between the insertion point and the second point determines the width of the paragraph.

Command: **MTEXT**
Attach/Rotation/Style/Height/Direction/ < Insertion Point > : *Select text insertion point*
Attach/Rotation/Style/Height/Direction/Width/2Points/ < Other corner > : **W**
Object width: **1.25**   *(Enter the paragraph width or specify the second point (@1.25,0))*

2Point

The 2Point option can be used to specify the width of the text paragraph by specifying any two points, regardless of the text insertion point.

Command: **MTEXT**
Attach/Rotation/Style/Height/Direction/ < Insertion Point > : *Select text insertion point*
Attach/Rotation/Style/Height/Direction/Width/2Points/ < Other corner > : **2P**
First point: **5,0**   *(Specify first point (5,0))*

Second point: **@1.25,0**   *(Specify the second point (@1.25,0))*

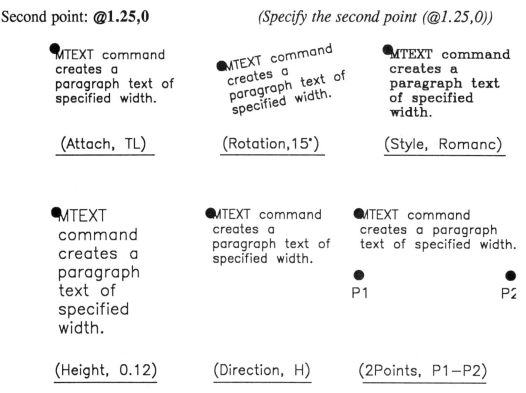

Figure 6-3 Attach options for text generated by MTEXT command

CHANGING MTEXT PROPERTIES (MTPROP Command)

Using MText Properties Dialogue Box

The **MText Properties** dialogue box can be invoked by entering **MTPROP** command at AutoCAD's Command: prompt. When you enter the command, AutoCAD will prompt you to select the text. Once the text is selected, the **MText Properties** dialogue box will be displayed on the screen. The dialogue box allows you to change the text style, text height, text direction, text attachment, text width, and text rotation. To change the text style, select the text or the arrow. AutoCAD will display a pop-up list of all defined text styles. You can Select a text style by clicking on the text style name in the pop-up list. Similarly, the direction and attachment can be changed by selecting the text or the arrow and then clicking on the desired

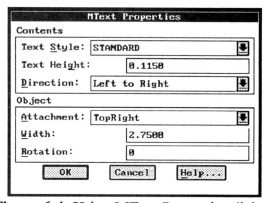

Figure 6-4 Using MText Properties dialogue box to change properties of MText

direction or text justification. The other values like text height, text width, and text rotation can be changed simply by entering a value in the corresponding edit boxes. Once you are done entering the new MText properties, select the OK button to exit the dialogue box. AutoCAD will update the properties of the selected MText object.

FORMATTING PARAGRAPH TEXT IN A TEXT EDITOR

The text can be formatted by entering the formatting codes in the text. To enter a paragraph text, you can use the text editor for DOS or use the text editor in Windows. With the formatting codes you can underline or overline a text string, create stacked text, or insert unbreaking space between two words. You can also use the formatting codes to change the color, font, text height, oblique angle, or the width of the text. The following is the list of the formatting codes for paragraph text:

\O...\o	Turns overline on and off	Turns \Ooverline\o on and off	Turns $\overline{\text{overline}}$ on and off
\L...\l	Turns underline on and off	Turns \Lunderline\l on and off	Turns underline on and off
\~	Inserts a nonbreaking space	Keeps the\~words together	Keeps the words together
\\	Inserts a backslash	Inserts \\ a backslash	Inserts \ a backslash
\{...\}	Inserts an opening and closing brace	This is \{bracketed\} word	The {bracketed} word
\Cvalue;	Changes to the specified color	Change \C1; the color	Change the color
\File name;	Changes to the specified font file	Chnage \Fromanc; this word	Change **this word**
\Hvalue;	Changes to the specified text height	Change \H0.15; this word	Change this word
\S...^...	Stacks the subsequent text at the \ or ^ symbol	2.005\S+0.001^−0.001	2.005$^{+0.001}_{-0.001}$
\Tvalue;	Adjusts the space between characters from .75 to 4 times	\T2;TRACKING	T R A C K I N G
\Qangle;	Changes obliquing angle	\Q15;OBLIQUE TEXT	*OBLIQUE TEXT*
\Wvalue;	Changes width factor to produce wide text	\W2;WIDE LETTERS	W I D E L E T T E R S
\P	Ends paragraph	First paragraph\PSecond paragraph	First paragraph Second paragraph

Figure 6-5 Formatting codes for paragraph text

Example

To paragraph text as shown in Figure 6-6 can be obtained by using the formatting codes as follows:

{\H0.15{\FROMANC;{\LNOTE\l}}}
{\FROMANC;Hardness} unless
otherwise specified
{\FROMANC;60RC}\S+3.0^-2.0

NOTE
Hardness unless
otherwise specified
+3.0
60RC−2.0

Figure 6-6 Using format codes for paragraph text

Note

Use the curly braces if you want to apply the format codes only to the text within the braces.

The curly braces can be nested up to eight levels deep.

TrueType Text Support

AutoCAD supports TrueType fonts. You can use your own TrueType fonts by adding them in the **Fonts** directory. You can also keep your fonts in a separate directory; in which case you must specify the location of your fonts directory in AutoCAD's search path.

The resolution and the text fill of the TrueType font text is controlled by TEXTFILL and TEXTQLTY system variables. If the TEXTFILL is set to 1, the text will be filled. If the value is set to 0, the text will not be filled. The TEXTQLTY variable controls the quality of the TrueType font text. The value of this variable can range from 0 to 100. The default value is 50, which gives a resolution of 300 DPI (Dots per inch). If the values is set to 100, the text will be drawn at 600 DPI. Higher the resolution, more time is takes to regenerate or plot the drawing.

Example
The following paragraph text used the TrueType font SWISS.TTF

{\H0.15{\FSWISS;{\LNOTE\l}}}
{\FSWISS;Hardness} unless
otherwise specified
{\FSWISS;60RC}\S+3.0^-2.0

NOTE
Hardness unless
otherwise specified
     +3.0
60RC−2.0

Figure 6-7 Using TrueType font to format paragraph text

EDITING MTEXT

The contents of a MText objects (Paragraph text) can be edited by using DDMODIFY and DDEDIT commands. You can also use AutoCAD's editing commands like MOVE, ERASE, ROTATE, COPY, MIRROR, and GRIPS to edit MText.

Editing MText Using DDMODIFY Command

When you enter DDMODIFY command, AutoCAD displays the **Modify MText** dialogue box on the screen. The text object that you select for editing is displayed in the **Contents** display box. If you select the **Edit Contents...** button, AutoCAD automatically switches to DOS editor where you can make any changes to the paragraph text. If you select **Edit Properties...** button, AutoCAD displays the **MText Properties** dialogue box. This dialogue box can be used to change the properties of the paragraph text as discussed earlier.

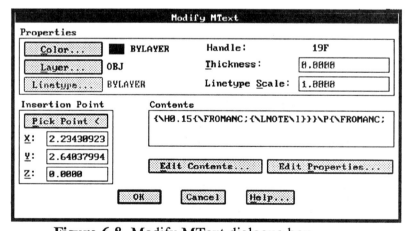

Figure 6-8 Modify MText dialogue box

Editing MTEXT Using DDEDIT Command

The paragraph text (MTEXT) can also be edited by using DDEDIT command. When you enter this command and select the paragraph text (MText) you want to edit, AutoCAD will automatically switch to DOS editor where you can edit the paragraph text.

CREATING PARAGRAPH TEXT FOR WINDOWS

If you are using Windows, you can create the paragraph text by selecting the Text button from the Draw toolbar or by entering MTEXT at Command prompt. Next, AutoCAD will prompt you to enter the insertion point and other corner of the paragraph text box. After entering these points, **Edit MText** dialogue box appears on the screen.

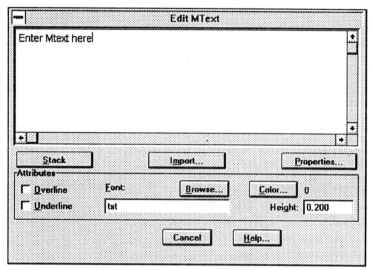

Figure 6-9 Edit MText dialogue box

Edit MTEXT Dialogue Box Options

The following is the description of different options available in Edit MTEXT dialogue box:

Text Box

The **Text Box** area displays the text that you enter. The width of the active text area is determined by the specified width of paragraph text.

Stack

The **Stack** option stacks the selected text. The text or fractions are stacked vertically.

Import

When you select this option, AutoCAD displays the **Import Text File** dialogue box. In this dialogue box you could select any file that you want to import in the Edit MTEXT dialogue box. The imported text is displayed in the text area. Note that only ASCII files are properly interpreted.

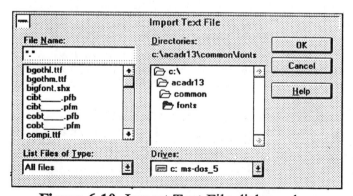

Figure 6-10 Import Text File dialogue box

Properties

When you select this option, AutoCAD displays the **MText Properties** dialogue box. You can use this dialogue box to change the text style, text height, direction, width, rotation, and attachment. For details, see "Changing MTEXT Properties" later in this section.

Attributes

Overline

If you click the overline button, it overlines the new or the selected text.

Underline

This button underlines the new or the selected text.

Font

You can specify the font by entering the font name (and path information) in the **Font** edit box. The selected font will be applied to the new text and the selected text.

Browse

If you select the Browse option, AutoCAD displays the **Change Font** dialogue box. You can use this dialogue box to browse through the font files and specify a font for the new text or change the font of the selected text. If the font is not recognized by windows, AutoCAD will display the **Select Font** dialogue box. You can select one of the supported fonts from the list.

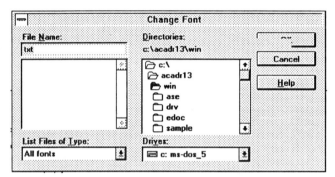

Figure 6-11 Change Font dialogue box

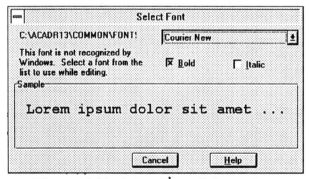

Figure 6-12 Select Font dialogue box

Color

If you select the **Color** button, AutoCAD displays the **Select Color** dialogue box. You can use this dialogue box to specify a color for the new text or change the color of the selected text.

Height

In the **Height** edit box, you can specify the text height of the new text or change the height of the selected text.

Changing MText Properties

You can change the MTEXT properties through **MText Properties** dialogue box. This box can be invoked by selecting the Properties button in the Edit MTEXT dialogue box or by entering MTPROP at AutoCAD Command: prompt.

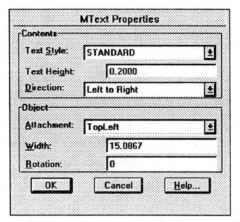

Figure 6-13 MText Properties dialogue box

Contents

Text Style
In the **Text Style** edit box you can specify the text style that you wan to use for new paragraph text.

Text Height
You can use the **Text Height** edit box to specify the text height for all text. The text height specified here becomes the default height for text, unless you override it by specifying a different height for the selected text.

Direction
The **Direction** option can be used to specify the direction in which the text must be read. Some languages like Chinese and Japanese are read from top to bottom, whereas English is read from left to right.

Object

Attachment
You can use the **Attachment** option to specify the text justification and text spill in relation to the text boundary.

Width
You can use the **Width** edit box to specify the horizontal width of the text boundary.

Rotation
You can use the **Rotation** edit box to specify the rotation angle of the text boundary.

Checking Spelling
You can check the spelling of text (text generated by TEXT, DTEXT, or MTEXT commands) by using the SPELL command. This command can be invoked from the pull-down menu (Select Tools/ Spelling), screen menu (Select TOOLS/ Spell:), or by entering SPELL command at AutoCAD Command: prompt.

Command: **SPELL**
Select object: *Select the text that you want to spell check*

If the spelling is not correct for any word in the selected text, AutoCAD displays the **Check Spelling** dialogue box. The mis-spelled word is displayed in the current word box and the correctly spelled alternate words are listed in the Suggestions box. You may select a word from the list, ignore the correction and continue with the spell check, or accept the change.

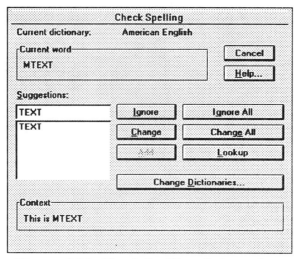

Figure 6-14 Check Spelling dialogue box

EXTERNAL REFERENCES

The Overlay Option

One of the problems with the XREF Attach option is that you cannot have circular reference. For example, let us assume that you are designing the plan layout of a manufacturing unit. One person is working on the floor plan and the second person is working on the furniture layout in the offices. The name of the drawings is FLOORPLN and OFFICES respectively. The person who is working on the office layout uses the XREF Attach option to insert the FLOORPLN drawing so that he has the latest floor plan drawing. The person who is working on the floor plan wants to XREF the OFFICES drawing. Now, if you use the XREF Attach option to reference the drawing,

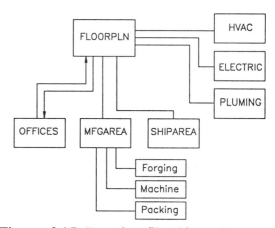

Figure 6-15 Drawing files hierarchy

AutoCAD displays an error message because by inserting the OFFICES drawing you are creating a circular reference. To overcome this problem, you can use the Overlay option to overlay the OFFICES drawing. This is a very useful option, because the Overlay option lets different operators share the drawing data without effecting your drawing.

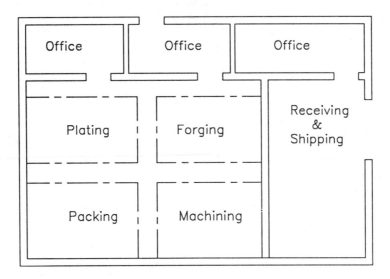

Figure 6-16 Sample plant layout drawing

Searching for External References

When you Xref a drawing, the path information is saved with the drawing. When you reload the drawing using XREF's Reload option or open the drawing, AutoCAD automatically loads the referenced drawing from the directory specified in the path. If the referenced drawing is not found in the specified path, then AutoCAD will automatically search the directories specified in the ACAD environment variable. The ACAD environment variable can be set by entering the following line at the system prompt or in the batch file that loads AutoCAD:

Set ACAD=C;\;C:\ACADR13\Support\;D:\Drawings\Proj1

In this environment variable definition it is assumed that the drawings are in Proj1 directory on D drive. If the referenced drawing is not found in the directory as specified in the path, then AutoCAD will search the file in the C drive root directory, ACADR13, Support, D drive root directory, Drawings, and Proj1 directories as defined in the environment variable.

Example

In this example you will use the XREF-Attach and XREF-Overlay to attach and reference the drawings. Two drawings PLAN and PLANFORG are given. The PLAN drawing consists of the floor plan layout and the PLANFORG drawing has the details of the forging section only. The CAD operator who is working on the PLANFORG drawing wants to XREF the PLAN drawing for reference. Also, the CAD operator working on the PLAN drawing should be able to XREF the PLANFORG drawing to complete the project. The following steps illustrate how to accomplish the defined task without creating a circular reference.

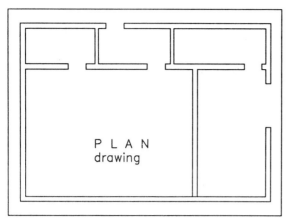

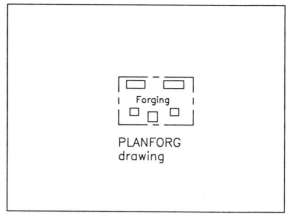

Figure 6-17 PLAN drawing

Figure 6-18 PLANFORG drawing

How is circular reference caused:

1. Load the drawing PLANFORG and use the XREF command to attach the PLAN drawing. Now, the drawing consists of PLANFORG and PLAN. Save the drawing.

2. Open the drawing file PLAN and use the XREF command to attach the PLANDWG drawing. AutoCAD will prevent you from attaching the drawing because it causes circular reference.

One possible solution is that the operator working on PLANFORG drawing detaches the PLAN drawing and then purges the block before saving it. This way the PLANFORG drawing does not contain any reference of PLAN drawing and would not cause any circular reference. The other solution is to use XREF's Overlay option as follows.

How to prevent circular reference:

1. Open the drawing PLANFORG and use the Overlay option of XREF command to overlay the PLAN drawing. The PLAN drawing is overlaid on the PLANFORG drawing.

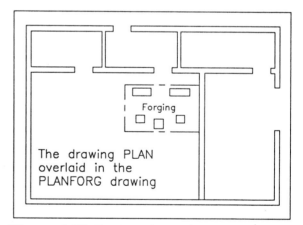

Figure 6-19 PLANFORG drawing

Figure 6-20 PLANFORG drawing after overlaying the PLAN drawing

2. Open the drawing file PLAN and use the Attach option of XREF command to attach the PLANFORG drawing. You will notice that only the PLANFORG drawing is attached. The drawing (PLAN) that was overlaid in the PLANFORG drawing does not appear in the current drawing.

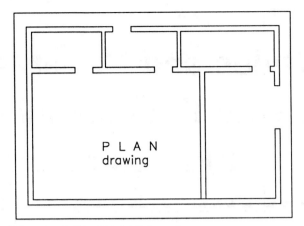
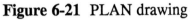

Figure 6-21 PLAN drawing

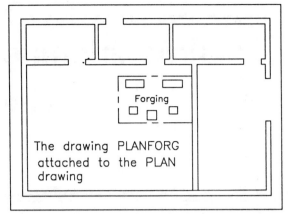

Figure 6-22 PLAN drawing after attaching the PLANFORG drawing

This way the CAD operator working on the PLANFORG drawing can overlay the PLAN drawing and the CAD operator working on the PLAN drawing can attach the PLANFORG drawing without causing a circular reference.

Dimensioning Styles and Variables
Geometric Dimensioning
and Tolerancing

7

USING STYLES AND VARIABLES
IN CONTROLLING DIMENSIONS

In AutoCAD the appearance of dimensions on the drawing screen and the manner in which they are saved in the drawing database is controlled by a set of dimension variables. The dimensioning commands use these variables as arguments. The variables that control the appearance of the dimensions can be managed with the dimension styles. With the use of **Dimension Style** dialogue box, you can control the dimension styles and dimension variables through a set of dialogue boxes. You can also do it by entering relevant commands at the Command: or Dim: prompts. This **Dimension Styles** dialogue box can be invoked from the pull-down menu (Select Data/ Dimension Style...) or screen menu (Select DATA/ DDim:). It can also be invoked by entering **DDIM** at AutoCAD's Command: prompt.

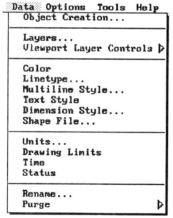

Figure 7-1 Selecting Dimension Style from the pull-down menu

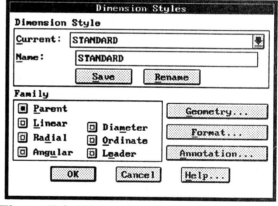

Figure 7-2 Dimension Styles dialogue box

CREATING AND RESTORING DIMENSION STYLES

Using Dialogue Box

The dimension style controls the appearance and positioning of the dimensions. In case the default dimensioning style (STANDARD) does not meet your requirements, you can select another dimensioning style or create one which meets your requirement. The default dimension style file name is **STANDARD**. The parent dimension styles can be created by entering the dimension style name in the **Name:** edit box (in **Dimension Styles** dialogue box) and then selecting the save button. The current dimension style name is listed in the **Current:** dimension styles list box. A style can be made current (restored) by picking the name of the dimension style that you want to make current from the list of defined dimension styles. The list of dimension styles can be displayed by picking the arrow in the **Current:** dimension styles list box. The dimension style name must not exceed 29 characters and the name should not end with a family member suffix code (See Using Dimension Style Families later in the chapter).

Using Command Line

You can also create dimension styles from the command line by entering DIMSTYLE at Command: prompt or by entering SAVE at Dim: prompt:

Command: **DIMSTYLE**
Dimension Style Edit (Save/Restore/STatus/Variables/Apply/?) <Restore>: **SAVE**
?/Name for new dimension style: *Enter the name of dimension style*

Command: **DIM**
Dim: **SAVE**
?/Name for new dimension style: *Enter the name of dimension style*

You can also restore the dimensions from the command line by entering **DIMSTYLE** at Command: prompt or by entering **RESTORE** at Dim: prompt.

Command: **DIMSTYLE**
Dimension Style Edit (Save/Restore/STatus/Variables/Apply/?) <Restore>: **RESTORE**
?/Enter dimension style name or RETURN to select dimension: *Enter the name of dimension style*

You can also select a dimension style by picking a dimension on a drawing. This can be accomplished by pressing the Enter key (null response) at the above prompt **?/Enter dimension style name or RETURN to select dimension:**. This way you can select the dimension style without knowing the name of the dimension style. Hence with the help of dimension styles, you can easily create and save groups of settings for as many types of dimensions as you require. Styles can be created to support almost any standards such as ANSI, DIN, ARCH.

GEOMETRY DIALOGUE BOX

The Geometry dialogue box can be used to specify the dimensioning attributes (variables) that effect the geometry of the dimensions. This dialogue box can be invoked by selecting the **Geometry** button in the **Dimension Styles** dialogue box. If the settings of the dimension variables have not been altered in the current editing session, the settings displayed in the dialogue box are the default settings.

Dimension Line

Suppress

The **Suppress:** check boxes control the drawing of the first and second dimension line. By default, both dimension lines will be drawn. You can suppress one or both dimension lines by selecting corresponding check boxes. The values of these check boxes are stored in DIMSD1 and DIMSD2 variables.

Note
The first and second dimension lines are determined by how you select the extension line origins. If the first extension line origin is on the right, then the first dimension line is also on the right.

Figure showing Geometry dialogue box:

```
┌────────────────────────────────────────────────────────────────┐
│                           Geometry                               │
│  Dimension Line                    Arrowheads                    │
│  Suppress:    □ 1st   □ 2nd         ┌─────────┐ ┌─────────┐      │
│  Extension:        [8.88]           │  ←───── │ │ ─────→  │      │
│  Spacing:          [0.25]       1st: [Closed Filled    ▼]        │
│  [Color...]     ■  BYBLOCK      2nd: [Closed Filled    ▼]        │
│                                 Size:      [8.89]                │
│  Extension Line                    Center                        │
│  Suppress:    □ 1st   □ 2nd      ☑ Mark                          │
│  Extension:        [0.07]        ☐ Line    ┌──────────┐          │
│  Origin Offset:    [0.03]        ☐ None    │    ⊕     │          │
│  [Color...]     ■  BYBLOCK       Size:     └──────────┘          │
│                                            [0.04]                │
│  Scale                                                           │
│  Overall Scale: [1.00000]        □ Scale to Paper Space          │
│                            [ OK ]   [ Cancel ]   [ Help... ]     │
└────────────────────────────────────────────────────────────────┘
```

Figure 7-3 Geometry dialogue box

Extension

The **Extension** (Oblique tick extension) edit box is used to specify the distance by which the dimension line will extend beyond the extension line. The Extension edit box can be used only when you have selected oblique arrowhead in the arrowhead pop-up list. The extension value entered in the Extension edit box gets stored in the DIMDLE variable. By default this edit box is disabled because the oblique arrowhead is not selected.

Spacing

The **Spacing** (Baseline Increment) edit box is used to control the dimension line increment (gap between successive dimension lines) for the continuation of a linear dimension drawn with the **Baseline** command. You can specify the dimension line increment to your requirement by entering the desired value in the **Spacing:** edit box. Also, when you are creating Continued dimensions with the **DIMContinue** command, the contents of **Spacing:** edit box specify the offset distance for the successive dimension lines, if needed to avoid drawing over the previous dimension line. The default value displayed in the **Spacing:** edit box is 0.38 units. The spacing (baseline increment) value is stored in the DIMDLI variable.

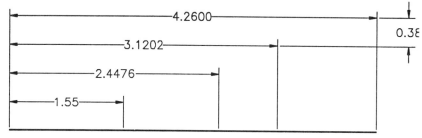

Baseline dimensioning with DIMDLI=0.38

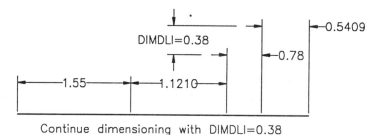

Continue dimensioning with DIMDLI=0.38

Figure 7-4 DIMDLI, Baseline increment

Dimension Line Color

Dimension arrows have the same color as that of the dimension line because arrows constitute a part of the dimension line. You can establish a color for the dimension line and the dimension arrows. The color number or the special color label gets stored in the DIMCLRD variable. The default color label for the dimension line is BYBLOCK. You can specify the color of the dimension line by selecting the Color... or the color swatch box. When you select these boxes, AutoCAD displays the Select Color dialogue box that you can use to specify a color. You can also enter the color name or color cumber in the color edit box.

Extension Lines

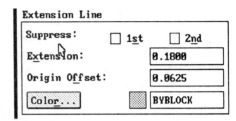

Suppress

The Suppress: check boxes control the display of the extension lines. By default, both extension lines will be drawn. You can suppress one or both extension lines by selecting corresponding check boxes. The values of these check boxes are stored in DIMSE1 and DIMSE2 variables.

Figure 7-5 Extension Line area of Geometry dialogue box

Note

The first and second extension lines are determined by how you select the extension line origins. If the first extension line origin is on the right, then the first extension line is also on right.

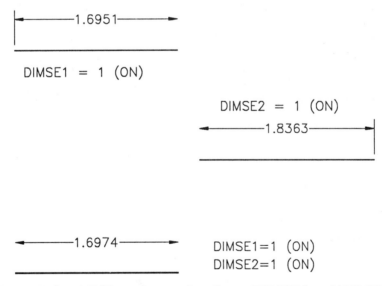

Figure 7-6 Visibility of extension lines, DIMSE1 and DIMSE2

Extension

Extension is the distance by which the extension line should extend past the dimension line. You can change the extension line offset by entering the desired distance value in the **Extension:** edit box. The value of this box is stored in the **DIMEXE** variable. The default value for extension distance is 0.1800 units.

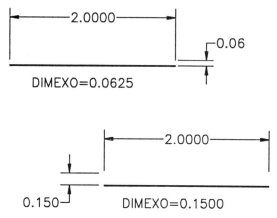

Figure 7-7 Origin offset, DIMEXO

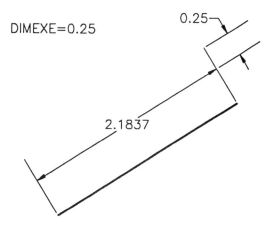

Figure 7-8 Extension above line, DIMEXE

Origin Offset

This edit box displays the distance value by which the extension lines are offset from the extension line origins you specify. You may have noticed that there exists a small space between the origin points you specify and the start of the extension lines. This space is due to specified offset. You can specify an offset distance of your choice by entering it in this box. AutoCAD stores this value in the **DIMEXO** variable. The default value for this distance is 0.0625.

Extension Line Color

In this box you can examine the existing extension lines color. The default extension lines color is BYBLOCK. You can change the color by assigning a new color to the extension lines. For example, if you want the extension lines color to be yellow, pick the color swatch box and select the desired color from the **Select Color** dialogue box. You can also specify the color by entering the color name or number in the color edit box. The color number or the color label is held in the DIMCLRE variable.

Arrowheads

1st: and 2nd: Pop-up boxes

When you create a dimension, AutoCAD draws the terminator symbols at the two ends of the dimension line. These terminator symbols, generally referred as arrowhead types, represent the start and end of a dimension. AutoCAD has provided seven standard termination symbols that you can apply at each end of the dimension line. In addition to these, you can also create your own arrows or terminator symbols. By default, the same arrowhead type is applied at both ends of the dimension line. If you

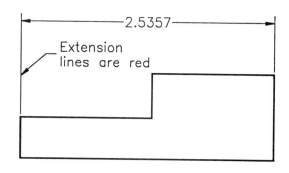

Figure 7-9 Changing extension line color, DIMCLRE

select the first arrowhead, it is automatically applied to the second by default. However, if you want to specify a different arrowhead at the second dimension line endpoint, then you must select the desired arrowhead type or user defined block from the second arrowhead list box.

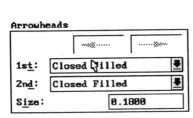

Figure 7-10 Arrowheads area of the Geometry dialogue box

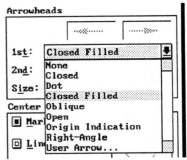

Figure 7-11 Arrowheads Pop-up list

The first endpoint of the dimension line is the intersection point of the first extension line and the dimension line. The first extension line is determined by the first extension line origin. However, in angular dimensioning the second end point is located in counterclockwise direction from the first point, regardless of how the points were selected when creating the angular dimension. the The specified arrowhead types are displayed in the arrowhead image box. The first arrowhead types is saved in DIMBLK1 and the second arrowhead type is saved in DIMBLK2 system variable. As mentioned earlier, by default arrows are drawn at the two end points of the dimension line. If you specify a different block instead of the arrowhead, the name of the block is stored in DIMBLK system variable.

User Arrow

If you want to specify a user defined block be drawn instead of the standard arrows at the ends of the dimension line, select the **User Arrow...** from the 1st or 2nd arrowheads Pop-up list to display the user arrow dialogue box. Enter the name of the pre-defined block name and then select the OK button. The size of the block is determined by the value stored in the Arrow Size edit box. In case there is no existing block by the name you specify, the message **"Can't find the arrow block"** is displayed in the lower left-hand corner of the dialogue box. The name of the block you select is stored in the DIMBLK1 or DIMBLK2 variable.

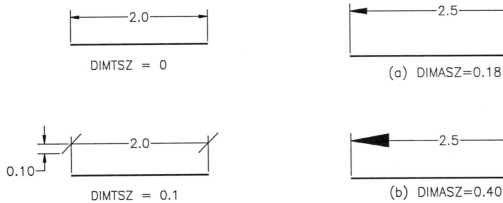

DIMTSZ = 0

DIMTSZ = 0.1

Figure 7-12 Tick marks are drawn if DIMTSZ is not zero

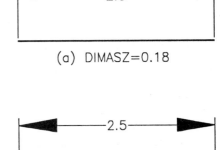

(a) DIMASZ=0.18

(b) DIMASZ=0.40

Figure 7-13 Controlling arrow size, DIMASZ

Size

Arrowheads and terminator symbols are drawn according to the size specified in the **Size:** edit box. The default value is 0.18 units. This value is stored in DIMASZ system variable. The arrowhead size value gets stored in the DIMASZ variable. By default the DIMTSZ set to 0 and DIMASZ is 0.18. The size of the ticks or arrowhead blocks is computed as DIMTSZ * DIMSCALE for ticks or DIMASZ*DIMSCALE for arrowhead blocks. Hence, if DIMSCALE factor is one, then the size of the tick is equal to the DIMTSZ value.

Scale

Overall Scale

The current general scaling factor that pertains to all the size related dimension variables like text size, center mark size, arrow size, etc. is displayed in the **Overall Scale:** edit box. You can alter the scaling factor to your requirement by entering the scaling factor of your choice in this box. Altering the contents of this box alters the value of the **DIMSCALE** variable since the current scaling factor is stored in it. The DIMSCALE is not applied to the measured lengths, coordinates, angles, or tolerances. The default value for this variable is 1.0; and in this case the dimensioning variables assume their preset values and the drawing is plotted at full scale. If the drawing is to be plotted at half the size, then the scale factor is the reciprocal of the drawing size. Hence the scale factor or the DIMSCALE value will be reciprocal of 1/2 which is 2/1 = 2.

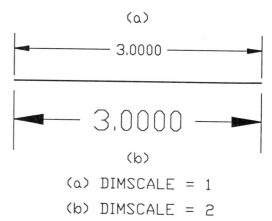

(a)

(b)

(a) DIMSCALE = 1

(b) DIMSCALE = 2

Figure 7-14 Using Overall Scaling to scale dimensions, DIMSCALE

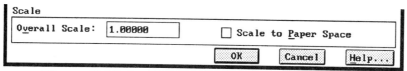

Figure 7-15 Scale area of Geometry dialogue box

Note
If you are in the middle of dimensioning process and you change the DIMSCALE value, only dimensions which will be drawn after the change has been made to the DIMSCALE variable will get affected.

Scale to Paper Space

If you select the **Scale to Paper Space** check box, the scale factor between the current model space viewport and paper space is automatically computed. Also, by selecting this check box the **Overall Scale:** edit box is disabled (it is grayed out in the dialogue box) and DIMSCALE is set to zero. When the DIMSCALE is assigned a value of 0.0, AutoCAD calculates an acceptable default value based on the scaling between the current model space viewport and paper space. If you are in paper space, or are not using the paper space feature, AutoCAD sets DIMSCALE to 1.0; else AutoCAD calculates a scale factor that makes it possible to plot text sizes, arrow sizes and other scaled distances at the values they have been previously set. (For further details see the "Model and Paper Space Dimensioning in "Editing Dimensions" chapter.)

Center

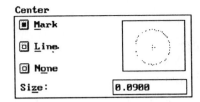

Figure 7-16 The Center area of the Geometry dialogue box

Mark

The **Size:** edit box in the Center area of the **Geometry** dialogue box displays the current size of center marks. The center marks are created by using **Center, Diameter,** and **Radius** dimensioning commands. The center marks are also created if you use the DIMCENTER command. In case of Radius and Diameter dimensioning, center mark is drawn only if the dimension line is located outside the circle or arc. You can specify the size of center mark by entering the required value in the **Size:** edit box. If you do not want a center mark, just enter 0 in the edit box or better select the **None** radio button. This value is stored in the DIMCEN variable. The default value in for DIMCEN is 0.09.

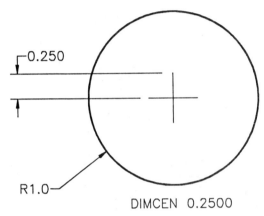

Figure 7-17 Center mark size, DIMCEN

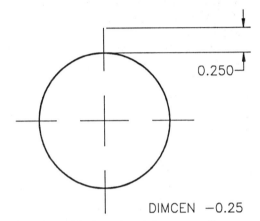

Figure 7-18 Mark with center lines, (Negative DIMCEN)

Line

If you want to draw center lines for a circle or arc, pick the **Line:** button. The value in the **Size:** edit box determines the size for the center lines as shown in Figure 7-18. The value you enter in the **Size:** edit box is stored as a negative value in the **DIMCEN** variable. In case of Radius and Diameter dimensioning, center lines are drawn only when the dimension line is located outside the circle or arc. The default setting is off (not checked), resulting in generation of dimensions without center lines.

None

If you select the **None** radio button, the center marks are not drawn and AutoCAD automatically disables the **Size:** edit box

Exercise 1

Draw the following figure and then set the values in the Geometry dialogue box to dimension the drawing as shown in the figure. (Dimension line spacing = 0.25, Extension line extension = 0.10, Origin offset = 0.05, Arrowhead size = 0.09). Assume the missing dimensions. (The drawing is shown on the next page.)

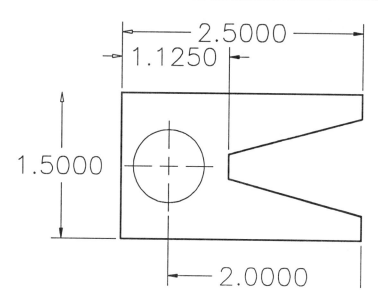

Figure 7-19 Drawing for Exercise 1

CONTROLLING DIMENSION FORMAT

You can control the dimension format through the **Format** dialogue box or assigning appropriate values to dimension variables. In dimension format you can control placement, horizontal justification, and vertical justification of dimension text. For example, you can force AutoCAD to align the dimension text along the dimension line. You can also force the dimension text to be displayed at the top of the dimension line. Some settings are interdependent. For example, if you select user defined option for text placement, the horizontal justification is automatically disabled. You can save the settings in a dimension style file for future use. The **Format** dialogue box has image tiles that update dynamically to display the text placement as the settings are changed. Individual items of the Format dialogue box and the relates dimension variables is described in the next section.

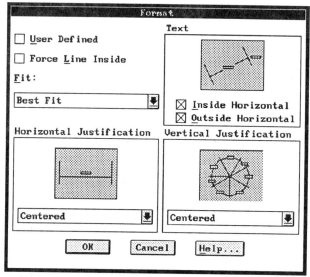

Figure 7-20 The Format dialogue box

User Defined

When you dimension, AutoCAD places the dimension text in the middle of the dimension line (If there is enough space). If you pick the **Used Defined** check box, you can position the dimension text anywhere along the dimension line. You will also notice that when you select this check box, the Horizontal Justification list box is automatically disabled.

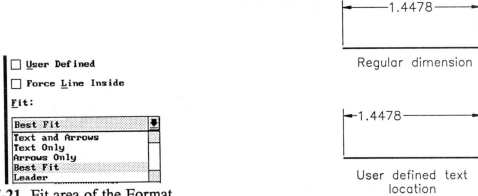

Figure 7-21 Fit area of the Format dialogue box

Figure 7-22 User defined dimension text position

Force Lines Inside

If the dimension text and the dimension lines are outside the extension lines and you want the dimension lines to be placed between the extension lines, pick the **Force Lines Inside** check box. The result of picking this box in Radius and Diameter dimensions (when Default text placement is horizontal) is that the dimension line and arrows are drawn inside the circle or arc, while the text and leader are drawn outside. When you select the **Force Line Inside** check box, the DIMTOFL variable is set **on** by AutoCAD. The default setting is off (not checked), resulting in generation of dimension line outside the extension lines when the dimension text is located outside the extension lines.

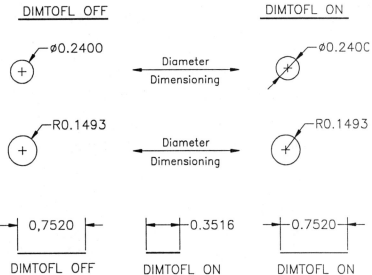

Figure 7-23 Force lines inside, DIMTOFL

Fit

When you select the down-arrow in the **Fit:** pop-up list, AutoCAD displays the available options for fitting the arrows and dimension text between the extension lines. The value of **Fit** option is stored in **DIMFIT** system variable. The following is the description of **Fit** options:

Text and Arrows

If you select this option, AutoCAD will place the arrows and dimension text between the extension lines if there is enough space available to fit both. Otherwise, both text and arrowheads are placed outside the extension lines. In this setting DIMFIT = 0

Text Only

When you select this option, AutoCAD places the text and arrowheads inside the extension lines if there is enough space to fit both. If space is not available for both arrows and text, the text is placed inside the extension lines and the arrows are placed outside the extension lines. If the there is not

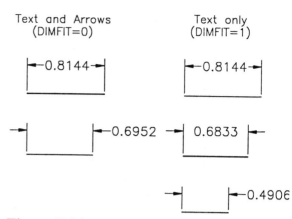

Figure 7-24 Text and Arrows and Text Only options

enough space for text, then both text and arrowheads are placed outside the extension lines. In this setting DIMFIT = 1

Text Only

When you select this option, AutoCAD places the text and arrowheads inside the extension lines if there is enough space to fit both. If space is not available for both arrows and text, the text is placed inside the extension lines and the arrows are placed outside the extension lines. If there is enough space to fit the arrows, then the arrows will be inside the extension lines and the dimension text outside the extension lines. If the there is not enough space for either text or arrowheads, then both text and arrowheads are placed outside the extension lines. In this setting DIMFIT = 2

Best Fit

This is the default option. In this option, AutoCAD places the dimension where it fits best between the extension lines. In this setting DIMFIT = 3

Leader

In this option, AutoCAD creates leader lines if there is not enough space available to fit the dimension text between the extension lines. The horizontal justification determines whether the text is placed to the right or the left of the leader. In this settings DIMFIT = 4

Horizontal Justification

The Horizontal Justification controls the placement of dimension text. To display the available options, select the down arrow in the pop-up list located just below the Horizontal Justification image tile. The selected setting is stores in DIMJUST system variable. The default option is Centered. The following is the list of the available options with DIMJUST values:

Options	Description	DIMJUST
Centered	The text between extension lines	0
1st Extension Line	Places text next to first extension line	1
2nd Extension Line	Places text next to second extension line	2
Over 1st Extension	Places the text aligned and above the first extension line	3
Over 2nd Extension	Places the text aligned and above the second extension line	3

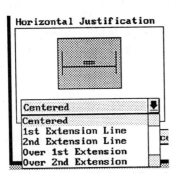

Figure 7-25 Horizontal Justification area of the Format dialogue box

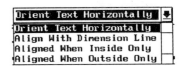

Figure 7-26 Using Horizontal Justification options to position text

Text

With the **Text** option you can specify the alignment of the dimension text with the dimension line. These options can be used to control the alignment of the dimension text for linear, radius, and diameter dimensions. By default the inside and outside dimension text is drawn horizontally.

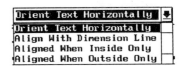

Figure 7-27 Controlling alignment of dimension text

Inside Horizontal

By default the dimension text is drawn horizontally with respect to the UCS (User Coordinate System). Therefore the **Inside Horizontal** check box is **on**. The alignment of the dimension line does not effect the text alignment. In this case DIMTIH variable is turned on. If you turn this check box off, the dimension text is aligned with the dimension line only when the dimension text is between the extension lines. By picking this option AutoCAD sets DIMTIH system variable **off**.

Outside Horizontal

By default the dimension text is drawn horizontally with respect to the UCS (User Coordinate System). Therefore the **Outside Horizontal** check box is **on**. The alignment of the dimension line does not effect the text alignment. If you turn this check box off, the dimension text is aligned with the dimension line only when the dimension text is outside the extension lines. Picking this option results in setting DIMTOH off.

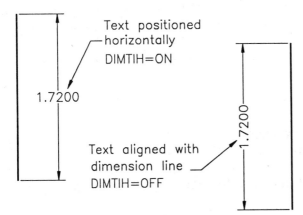

Figure 7-28 Dimension text inside horizontal, DIMTIH

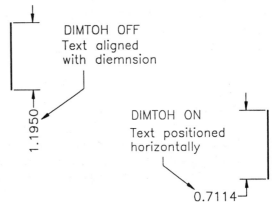

Figure 7-29 Dimension text outside horizontal, DIMTOH

Vertical Justification

Just as the Horizontal pop-up list controls the horizontal placement of the dimension text, **Vertical** pop-up list controls the vertical placement of the dimension text. The present setting will be highlighted. The controlling of the vertical placement of dimension text is possible only when the dimension text is drawn in its normal (default) location. This setting is stored in DIMTAD system variable. Following are the vertical text placement settings:

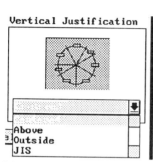

Figure 7-30 Controlling vertical justification

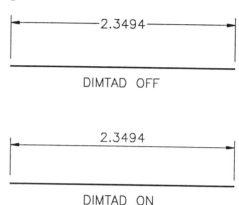

Figure 7-31 Using Centered justification to place text above dimension line, DIMTAD

Centered

If this option is picked, the dimension text gets centered on the dimension line in such a way that the dimension line is split to allow the placement of the text. Picking of this option sets DIMTAD off. In this setting DIMTAD = 0

Above

If this option is picked, the dimension text is placed above the dimension line, except when the dimension line is not horizontal and the dimension text inside the extension lines is horizontal (DIMTIH=1). The distance of the dimension text from the dimension line is controlled by the DIMGAP value. This results in an unbroken solid dimension line drawn under the dimension text. In this setting DIMTAD = 1

Outside

This option places the dimension text on the side of the dimension line. In this setting DIMTAD = 2

JIS

This option lets you place the dimension text to conform to JIS representation. In this setting DIMTAD = 3

Exercise 2

Draw the following figure and then set the values in the Geometry and Format dialogue boxes to dimension the drawing as shown in the figure. (Dimension line spacing = 0.25, Extension line extension = 0.10, Origin offset = 0.05, Arrowhead size = 0.09). Assume the missing dimensions and set DIMTXT = 0.09. (The drawing is shown on the next page.)

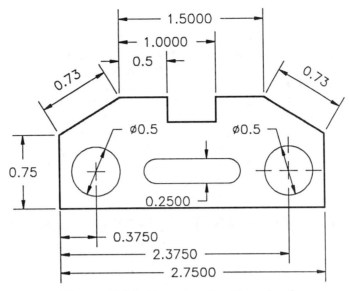

Figure 7-32 Drawing for Exercise 2

ANNOTATION DIALOGUE BOX

You can use the **Annotation** dialogue box to control the dimension text format. AutoCAD lets you attach the user defined prefix or suffix to the dimension text. For example, you can define the diameter symbol as prefix by entering %%C in the Prefix edit box; AutoCAD will automatically attach the diameter symbol in front of the dimension text. Similarly, you can define unit type like **mm** as suffix. By defining this as suffix, AutoCAD will attach **mm** at the end of every dimension text. This dialogue box also enables you to define tolerances, alternate units, zero suppression, and dimension text format.

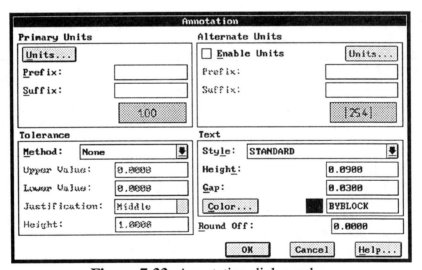

Figure 7-33 Annotation dialogue box

Primary Units

The primary units area of the **Annotation** dialogue box consists of Units, Prefix, and Suffix. It also has a image tile that displays the current dimension text format. If you pick this image tile, AutoCAD cycles the displayed value through different tolerance methods. The following is the description of Units, Prefix, and Suffix options:

Units:

When you select the **Units...** box, AutoCAD displays the **Primary Units** dialogue box. You can use this dialogue box to control Units for Linear and Angular measurements, Dimension Precision for linear and angular, and Zero Suppression for linear and angular measurements. If you select the down arrow in the **Units** pop-up list, AutoCAD displays the unit formats like Decimal, Scientific, Architectural, etc. You can select one of the listed units that you want to use when dimensioning. Notice, by selecting a dimension unit format, the drawing units (that you might have selected by using DDUNITS or UNITS command) are not affected. You can also control the unit precision by using the Precision: pop-up list. The units setting for linear dimensions is stored in DIMUNIT system variable, unit setting for angular dimensions in DIMAUNIT, setting of precision.(number of decimal places) in DIMDEC, and the setting of precision for tolerance (number of decimal places for tolerance) in DIMTDEC.

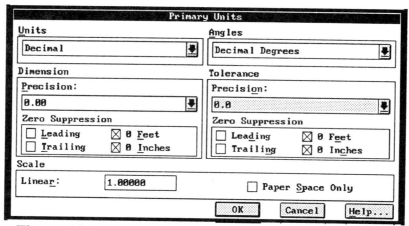

Figure 7-34 Primary Units dialogue box for dimensioning

Zero Suppression

If you want to suppress the feet portion of a feet-and-inches dimension when the distance is less than one foot (when there is a zero in the feet portion of the text), pick the **0 Feet** check box. For example, if you pick the 0 Feet check box, the dimension text 0'-8 3/4" becomes 8 3/4". By default 0 Feet and 0 Inches value is suppressed. If you want to suppress the inches part of a feet-and-inches dimension when the distance in the feet portion is an integer number and the inches portion is zero, pick the **0 Inches** check box. For example, if you pick the 0 Inches check box, the dimension text 3'-0" becomes 3".

If you want to suppress the leading zeros in all the distances measured in decimals, check the **Leading check** box. For example, by picking this box, 0.0750 becomes .0750. If you want to suppress the trailing zeros in all the distances measured in decimals, check the **Trailing** check box. For example, by picking this box, 0.0750 becomes 0.075. Trailing zeros are of significance to the tolerance and hence they should be edited keeping in mind the degree of accuracy required in the dimension tolerance. AutoCAD stores zero suppression as an integer value in the DIMZIN variable in the following manner:

If you pick the 0 Feet check box an integer value 3 is stored in DIMZIN variable by AutoCAD. If you pick the 0 Inches check box an integer value 2 is stored in DIMZIN variable by AutoCAD. If you pick the Leading check box an integer value 4 is stored in DIMZIN variable by AutoCAD. If you pick the Trailing check box an integer value 9 is stored in DIMZIN variable by AutoCAD. A combination of not picking the 0 Feet and 0 Inches check boxes results in the display of the zero feet as well as the zero inches of a measurement. For this combination, the value stored in DIMZIN is 1.

Remember that by default, the 0 Feet and 0 Inches check boxes are active (selected, picked). This is displayed by a cross mark in these two check boxes. The table below shows the result of selecting one of the DIMZIN values:

Scale

You can specify a global scale factor for linear dimension measurements by entering the desired scale factor in the **Linear** edit box. All the linear distances measured by dimensions, which includes radii, diameters, and coordinates, are multiplied by the existing value in the Linear scaling edit box. The angular dimensions are not effected. In this manner the value of the Linear scaling factor affects the content of the default (original) dimension text. Default value for the Linear scaling is 1. With the default value the dimension text generated is the actual measurement of the entity being dimensioned. The Linear scaling value is saved by AutoCAD in **DIMLFAC** variable.

Note

The linear scaling value is not exercised on rounding value or plus or minus tolerance values. Therefore, if you change the linear scaling factor, the tolerance values are not affected.

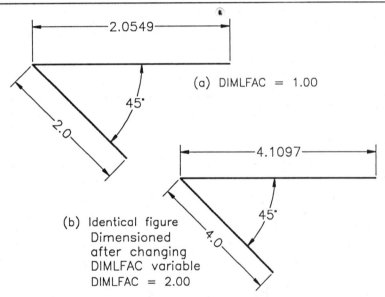

Figure 7-35 Changing dimension length scaling factor, DIMLFAC

Text Prefix

You can append a prefix to the dimension measurement by entering the desired prefix in the **Prefix:** edit box. The dimension text gets converted into the **Prefix < dimension measurement >** format. For example, if you enter the text "Ht" in the text Prefix edit box, the text "Ht" will be places in front of the dimension text. AutoCAD saves the prefix string in the **DIMPOST** system variable.

Note

Once you specify a prefix, the default prefixes such as "R" in radius dimensioning and "ϕ" in diameter dimensioning are cancelled.

Text Suffix

Just like appending a prefix, you can append a suffix to the dimension measurement by entering the desired suffix in the **Suffix** edit box. For example, if you enter the text "cm" in the Text Suffix edit box, the dimension text will have <dimension measurement>cm format. In case tolerances are enabled (DIMTOL is on), the specified suffix gets appended to the main dimension as well as to the upper and lower tolerances values. AutoCAD stores the suffix string in the **DIMPOST** variable.

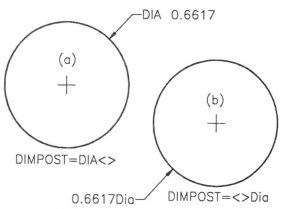

Figure 7-36 Using text prefix and text suffix in dimensioning, DIMPOST

Tolerances

The **Tolerance** area of the **Annotation** dialogue box lets you specify the tolerance method, tolerance value, justification of tolerance text, and the height of the tolerance text. For example, if you do not want a dimension to deviate more than plus 0.01 and minus 0.02, you can specify it by selecting **Deviation** from the **Method:** pop-up list and then specify the plus and minus deviation in the **Upper Value:**

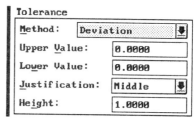

Figure 7-37 Tolerance area of Annotation dialogue box

and the **Lower Value:** edit boxes. When you dimension, AutoCAD will automatically append the tolerance to the dimension. Different settings and their effect on relevant dimension variables are explained in the following sections:

Method

The **Method:** pop-up list lets you select the tolerance method. The tolerance methods supported by AutoCAD are Symmetrical, Limits, Deviation, and Basic. The following is the description of these tolerance methods:

Symmetrical

If you select **Symmetrical**, the Lower Value: edit box is disabled and the value specified in the Upper Value: edit box is applied to both plus and minus tolerance. For example, if the value specified in the Upper Value edit box is 0.05. The tolerance appended to the dimension text is ± 0.05.

Deviation

If you select the **Deviation** tolerance method, the values in the **Upper Value** and **Lower Value** edit boxes will be displayed as plus and minus dimension tolerances. In case the Upper Value: and the Lower: Value edit boxes contain identical values (both plus and minus tolerances are same), AutoCAD draws a ± symbol followed by the tolerance value when the dimension is drawn. For example, if you enter 0.50 in both the edit boxes the resulting dimension text generated will have the format <dimension measurement> ±0.50.

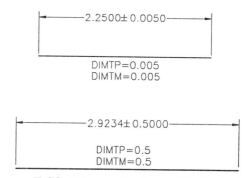

Figure 7-38 Dimensioning with deviation tolerance (when upper value = lower value)

If you do not enter identical values for the plus and minus tolerances, AutoCAD appends a plus sign (+) to the positive values of the tolerance and a negative (-) sign to the negative values of tolerance. For example, if the upper value of the tolerance is 0.005, and the lower value of the tolerance is 0.002, the resulting dimension text generated will have a positive tolerance of 0.0050 and a negative tolerance of 0.002:

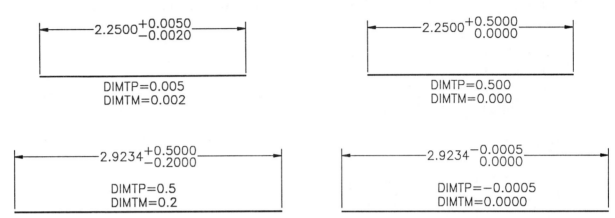

Figure 7-39 Dimensioning with deviation tolerance (when upper value is not equal to lower value)

Figure 7-40 Dimensioning with deviation tolerance

If one of the tolerance values is zero, no sign is appended to it. On picking the deviation tolerance, AutoCAD sets **DIMTOL** variable on and **DIMLIM** variable off. The values in the Upper Value and Lower Value edit boxes are saved in the **DIMTP** and **DIMTM** system variables respectively.

Limits

If you pick the **Limits** tolerance method from the Method: pop-up list, AutoCAD adds the upper value (contents of **Upper Value** edit box) to the dimension text (actual measurement) and subtracts the lower value (contents of the **Lower Value** edit box) from the dimension text. The resulting values are drawn with the dimension text. Selecting **Limits** tolerance method results in setting the **DIMLIM** variable on and the **DIMTOL** variable off. The numeral values in the Upper Value and Lower Value edit boxes are saved in the **DIMTP** and **DIMTM** system variables respectively.

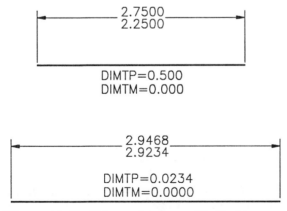

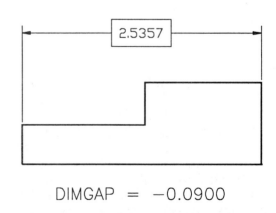

Figure 7-41 Dimensioning with limits tolerance

Figure 7-42 Basic dimension (DIMGAP assigned a negative value)

Basic

A basic dimension text is the dimension text with a box drawn around it. The main use of Reference dimensions is in Geometric Dimensioning and Tolerance. The basic dimension can be realized by picking the basic tolerance method. The Basic dimension is also called a Reference dimension. The distance provided around the dimension text (distance between dimension text and the lines of the rectangular box) is held as a negative value in the **DIMGAP** variable. The negative value signifies basic dimension. The default setting is off (not checked), resulting in generation of dimensions without the box around the dimension text.

None

If you select None in the Method: pop-up list, AutoCAD disables the **Tolerance** area of Annotation dialogue box. By doing so, no tolerances are appended to dimensions.

Justification

The **Justification** lets you justify the dimension tolerance text. Three justifications are possible, Bottom, Middle, and Top. If you select Limits tolerance method, the Justification pop-up list is automatically disabled. The settings are saved in **DIMTOLJ** system variable (Bottom = 0, Middle = 1, and Top = 2).

Height

The **Height** edit box lets you specify the height of the dimension tolerance text relative to the dimension text height. The default value is 1; the height of tolerance text is same as the dimension text height. If you want the tolerance text to be seventy five percent of dimension height text, enter 0.75 in the Height edit box. The ratio of the tolerance height to the dimension text height is calculated by AutoCAD and then stored in the DIMTFAC variable.

DIMTFAC = Tolerance Height / Text Height

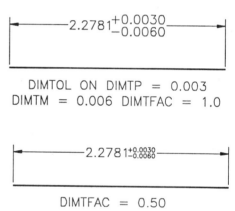

Figure 7-43 Tolerance Height, DIMTFAC

Alternate Units

By default the Alternate Units area is disabled and the value of **DIMALT** variable set off. If you want to perform alternate units dimensioning, pick the **Enable Units** check box. Doing so, AutoCAD activates the Units..., Prefix, and Suffix edit boxes. If you select the **Units...** box, AutoCAD displays the **Alternate Units** dialogue box that is identical to **Primary Units** dialogue box discussed earlier. In this dialogue box you can specify the values that will be applied only to alternate dimensions. In order

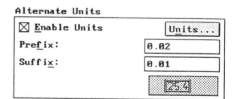

Figure 7-44 Alternate Units area of Annotation dialogue box

to generate a value in the alternate system of measurement, a factor with which all the linear dimensions will be multiplied is needed. The value for this factor can be entered in the Linear: edit box located in the Scale area of the Alternate Units dialogue box.

Suffixes can be appended to all types of dimensions except angular dimensions. The figure shown illustrates the result of entering information in the Alternate Units area. The decimal places get saved in DIMALTD variable, the scaling value (contents of Linear edit box) in the DIMALTF variable, angle format for angular dimensions in DIMAUNIT, and the suffix string (contents of Suffix edit box) in the DIMAPOST variable. Similarly, number of decimal places for the tolerance value of an alternate dimension is stored in DIMALTTD, suppression of zeros for tolerance values in DIMALTTZ, units format for alternate units in DIMALTU, and suppression of zeros for alternate unit decimal values in DIMALTZ.

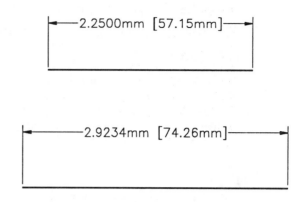

Figure 7-45 Dimensioning with alternate units

Text

The **Text** area of Annotation dialogue box lets you specify the text style, text height, text gap, and the color of the dimension text. The following is the description of these options:

Style:

If you pick the down arrow in the **Style:** pop-up list, AutoCAD displays the names of the pre-defined text styles. From this list you can pick the style name that you want to use

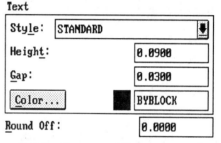

Figure 7-46 Alternate Units area of Text Format dialogue box

for dimensioning. You must define the text style before you can use it in dimensioning (See the STYLE command). The value of this setting is stored in **DIMTXSTY** system variable. The change in dimension text style does not effect the text style that you are using to draw the text.

Text Height

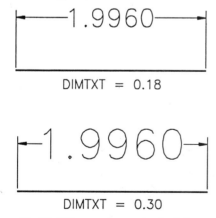

Figure 7-47 Dimension text height, DIMTXT

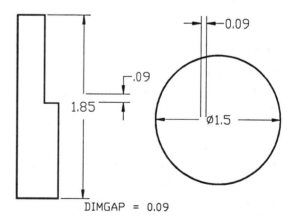

Figure 7-48 Text gap, DIMGAP

You can customize the height of the dimension text to your requirement by entering the required text height in the **Height:** edit box. The changing of the dimension text height is possible only when the current text style does not have a fixed height. In other words, the text height specified in the **STYLE** command should be zero because a predefined (specified in the **STYLE** command) text height overrides any other setting for the dimension text height. The value in the Height edit box gets stored in the **DIMTXT** variable. The default text height is 0.1800 units.

Text Gap

The **Gap:** edit box is used to specify the distance between the dimension line and the dimension text. You can enter a text gap of your requirement in this edit box. Text Gap value is also used as the measure of minimum length for the segments of the dimension line and in basic tolerance. The default value specified in this box is 0.09 units. The value of this setting is stored in **DIMGAP** system variable.

Note
*You cannot enter a negative value in the "Text Gap" box. Once the "**Basic dimension**" check box is picked, the negative value is stored in the DIMGAP variable.*

Dimension Text Color

A color can be assigned to the dimension text by specifying it in the **Color:** edit box. The color number or special color label is held in the **DIMCLRT** variable. The default color label is BYBLOCK. Selection of colors has been described in detail earlier in this chapter (See Dimension line, Color in Geometry dialogue box).

Round Off

If you want to round off the dimension distances to some value, you can do it by entering the value in the **Round Off:** edit box. For example, if you want to round off all distances to the nearest 0.25 units, enter 0.25 in the Round Off edit box. The default value for Round Off is 0; with this value rounding does not take place. The round off value does not effect the angular dimensions. The rounding value is saved in the **DIMRND** variable.

Note
The precision value set by the DDUNITS command governs the number of digits which lie on the right of the decimal point. DIMRND is independent of the precision value set for the drawing.

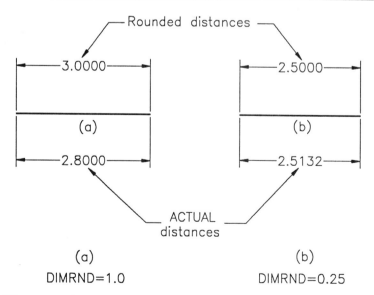

Figure 7-49 Rounding dimension measurements, DIMRND

Exercise 3

Draw the following figure and then set the values in the Geometry, Format, and Annotation dialogue boxes to dimension it as shown in the figure. (Dimension line spacing = 0.25, Extension line extension = 0.10, Origin offset = 0.05, Arrowhead size = 0.09, Dimension text height = 0.09). Assume the missing dimensions.

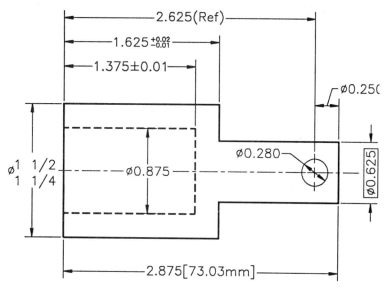

Figure 7-50 Drawing for Exercise 3

Redefinition of Dimension (DIMSHO)

The associative dimension compute dynamically as the dimension is dragged. This feature is controlled by DIMSHO system variable. By default it is **On**, which means that redefinition of the dimension will take place as it is dragged. Although it is a good feature, sometimes the dynamic dragging can be very slow. In that case you can turn it off by setting DIMSHO to **Off**. When you dimension a circle or an arc, the setting of DIMSHO is ignored.

Positioning Dimension Text (DIMUPT)

When you draw a dimension and define the location of the dimension line, AutoCAD draws the dimension lines and places the dimension text in the middle of the dimension line. This setting is saves in the **DIMUPT** system variable. The default value of this variable is **Off**. If you set the DIMUPT variable On, AutoCAD will place the dimension text at the point that you have specified as dimension line location. This enables you to position the dimension text anywhere along the dimension line.

DIMENSION STYLE FAMILIES

The dimension style feature of AutoCAD lets the user define a dimension style with the values that are common to all dimensions. For example, the arrow size, dimension text height, or the color of dimension line are generally same in all types of dimensioning like linear, radial, diameter, angular, etc. You can say that these dimensioning types belong to same family because they have some characteristics that are common. In AutoCAD this is called a **Dimension Style Family**, and the values assigned to the family are called **Dimension Style Family Values**.

After you have defined the Dimension Style Family Values, you can specify variation on it for other types of dimension like radial, diameter, etc. For example, in radial dimensioning if you want to limit the number of decimal places to 2, you can specify that value for radial dimensioning. The other values will stay the same as the family values to which this dimension type belongs. When you use the radial dimension, AutoCAD automatically uses the style that was defined for radial dimensioning, otherwise it creates a radial dimension with the values as defined for the family. After you have created and saved a Dimension Family Style, any changes in the parent style are not applied to family members. Special suffix codes are appended to the Family dimension style name that correspond to different dimension types. For example, if the family dimension style name is MYSTYLE and you defines a diameter type of dimension, AutoCAD will append $4 at the end of the Family Dimension style name. The name for the diameter type of dimension will be MYSTYLE$4. The following are the suffix codes for different types of dimensioning:

Suffix Code	Dimension Type	Suffix Code	Dimension Type
0	Linear	2	Angular
3	Radius	4	Diameter
6	Ordinate	7	Leader

The following example illustrates the concepts of Family Style dimensioning:

Example 1

In this example you will perform the following tasks:
1. Specify the values for Dimension Style Family.
2. Specify the values for linear type dimension.
3. Specify the values for diameter type dimension.
4. After saving the dimension style, you will use it to dimension the given drawing.

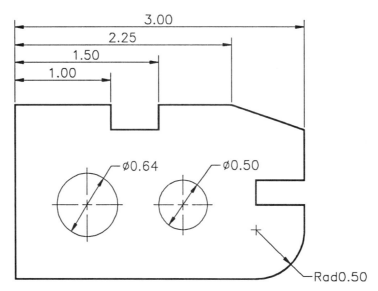

Figure 7-51 Dimensioning using Dimension Style Families

Step 1
Invoke the Dimension Styles dialogue box by entering DDIM command at AutoCAD Command: prompt. You can also invoke it from the pull-down menu (Select Data/ Dimension Style) or from the screen menu (Select DRAW DIM/ DDim:). If you have not defined any dimension style, AutoCAD will display STANDARD in the Current: edit box. If it does not, select the STANDARD style from the pop-up list.

Step 2

Select the parent button (If it is not already selected) and then select the Geometry button to invoke the **Geometry** dialogue box. In this dialogue box change the following values.

Spacing	**0.15**	**Extension**	**0.07**	**Origin Offset**	**0.03**
Arrow Size	**0.09**	**Center Size**	**0.05**		

Select the OK button to exit the Geometry dialogue box and then select Annotation button to invoke the **Annotation** dialogue box. In this dialogue box change the following values:

Text Height	**0.09**	**Text Gap**	**0.03**

After entering the values select the OK button to return to Dimension Styles dialogue box. In the Name: edit box enter the name of the dimension style, MYSTYLE. Select the Save button to save the dimension style file (MYSTYLE). This dimension style file contains the values that are common to all dimensions types.

Step 3

From the Dimension Styles dialogue box select the Linear radio button and then select the Format button. In the Format dialogue box set the following values.

1. Turn off the Inside Horizontal and Outside Horizontal check boxes.
2. In the Vertical Justification select **Above**.

Select the OK button to return to Dimension Styles dialogue box. From this box select the Annotation button to display the **Annotation** dialogue box. In this dialogue box change the following values:

1. Decimal Units.
2. Dimension Precision to two places of decimal.
3. Tolerance precision to two places of decimal.

Select the OK button to return to Annotation dialogue box. Select the OK button again to return to Dimension Styles dialogue box. Select the Save button to save the changes.

Step 4

In the Dimension Styles dialogue box select the Diameter radio button and then select the Format button. In the Format dialogue box select the **User Defined** check box. Select the OK button to return to Dimension Styles dialogue box. In this dialogue box select the Annotation button. In the Annotation dialogue box select the Units button and set the precision to two places of decimal. Return to Dimension Styles dialogue box. Select the Save button to save the changes. Select the OK button to exit from the Dimension Styles dialogue box.

Step 5

Use the DIMLIN and DIMBASE command to draw the linear dimensions as shown in the figure. Notice that when you enter any linear dimensioning command, AutoCAD automatically uses the values that were defined for Linear type of dimensioning.

Step 6

Use the DIMDIA command to dimension the circles as shown in the figure. Again notice that the dimensions are drawn according to the values specified for Diameter type of dimensioning.

Step 7

Now define the values for the Radial type of dimensioning and then dimension the arc as shown in the figure. Good luck!

USING DIMENSION STYLE OVERRIDES

In a production drawing most of the dimension characteristics are common. The values that are common to different dimensioning types can be defined in the dimension style family. However, at times you might have dimensions that are different. For example, you may need two types of linear dimensioning; one with tolerance and one without tolerance. One way to draw these dimensions is to create two dimensioning styles. You can also use the dimension variable overrides to override the existing values. For example, you can define a dimension style (MYSTYLE) that draws dimensions without tolerance. Now, to draw a dimension with tolerance or update an existing dimension, you can override the previously defined value. You can override the values through the Dimension Styles dialogue box or by setting the variable values at Command prompt. The following example illustrates how to use the dimension style overrides.

Example 2

In this example you will update the 3.00 dimension so that the tolerance is displayed with the dimension. You will also add two linear dimensions as shown in the figure.

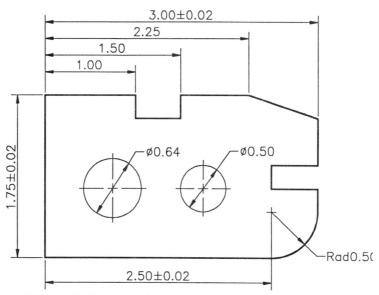

Figure 7-52 Overriding the dimension style values

Using Dimension Styles

Step 1
Invoke the Dimension Styles dialogue box and select the Annotation button to display the Annotation dialogue box. In this dialogue box specify the tolerance, symmetrical with upper value 0.02. Select the OK button to exit the dialogue box. Notice the current style has changed to +MYSTYLE, indicating that override exists for MYSTYLE dimension style. If you override another value or any number of values, they will be saved in +MYSTYLE. AutoCAD does not create additional files to store other overridden values.

Step 2
Use the DIMSTYLE command to apply the change to the existing dimensions.

    Command: **DIMSTYLE**
    Dimension Style Edit (Save/Restore/STatus/Variables/Apply/?) <Restore>: **A**
    Select objects: *Select the dimensions that you want to update*

After you select the dimension, AutoCAD will update the dimension and the tolerance will be appended to the selected dimension. If you create a new dimension, the tolerance value will be automatically displayed with the dimension, unless you make DIMSTYLE (Dimension style) current. This is not possible if you override a dimension style value using other commands like DDMODIFY or DIMOVERRIDE.

Using DDMODIFY Command

Step 1
You can also use the DDMODIFY command to modify a dimension. Enter DDMODIFY at Command prompt and select the dimension that you want to modify.

Command: **DDMODIFY**
Select object to modify: *Select the dimension*

Step 2
After you select the dimension, AutoCAD will display the Modify Dimension dialogue box. From this dialogue box select the Annotation button to display the Annotation dialogue box. Specify the tolerance for linear dimension; Symmetrical with Upper Value 0.02. Select the OK button to exit Annotation and Modify Dimension dialogue boxes. The dimension will be updated to new specifications.

Using DIMOVERRIDE Command

Step 1
You can also DIMOVERRIDE command to override a dimension value. If you want to have tolerance displayed with the dimension, make sure the tolerances are specified. Use the following command to specify the tolerance:

Command: **DIMTP**
The value for DIMTP <0.0000>:): 0.02

Command: **DIMTM**
The value for DIMTM <0.0000>:): 0.02

Step 2
Use the DIMOVERRIDE command to override the selected dimension.

Command: **DIMOVERRIDE**
Dimension variable to override (or Clear to remove overrides): **DIMTOL**
Current value <off> New value: **ON**
Dimension variable to override: ◄─┘
Select objects: *Select the object that you want to update*

You can also update a dimension by entering **Update** at **Dim:** prompt. For details see the chapter "Editing Dimensions"

COMPARING AND LISTING DIMENSION STYLES
(DIMSTYLE Command)

The Save, Restore, and Apply option of DIMSTYLE command have been discussed earlier in this chapter. You can also use this command to obtain the status of a dimension style or compare a dimension style with the current style.

Comparing Dimension Styles

You can compare the current dimension style with another style by appending the tilde (˜) symbol in front of the dimension style name.

Command: **DIMSTYLE**
Dimension Style Edit (Save/Restore/STatus/Variables/Apply/?) <Restore>: **R**
?/Enter dimension style name or RETURN to select dimension: **˜Standard**

AutoCAD will display a listing of dimension variable names and their values for the Standard dimension style and the current dimension style. Only those variables are listed that have different values in the current and the named styles.

Listing Dimension Styles

The **STatus** option of **DIMSTYLE** command displays the **current** dimensioning status. You can also use the question mark (**?**) to display the named dimension styles in the current drawing.

Command: **DIMSTYLE**
Dimension Style Edit (Save/Restore/STatus/Variables/Apply/?) <Restore>: **ST or ?**

If you select the **Variables** option, AutoCAD will display the dimension status of the named dimension style or the dimension style that is associated with the selected dimension.

Command: **DIMSTYLE**
Dimension Style Edit (Save/Restore/STatus/Variables/Apply/?) <Restore>: **V**
?/Enter dimension style name or RETURN to select dimension: **MYSTYLE**

USING EXTERNALLY REFERENCED DIMENSION STYLES

The externally referenced dimensions cannot be used directly in the current drawing. When you XREF a drawing, the drawing name is appended to the style name and the two are separated by the vertical bar (|) symbol. It uses the same syntax as other externally dependent symbols. For example, if the drawing (FLOOR) has a dimension style called DECIMAL and you Xref this drawing in the current drawing, AutoCAD will rename the dimension style to FLOOR|DECIMAL. You cannot make this dimension style current and you cannot modify it either. However, you can use it as a template to create a new style. To accomplish this, invoke the **Dimension Styles** dialogue box and make the FLOOR|DECIMAL style current. In the **Name:** edit box enter the name of the dimension style and save it. AutoCAD will create a new dimension style with the same values as that of the externally referenced dimension style (FLOOR|DECIMAL).

GEOMETRIC DIMENSIONING AND TOLERANCING

One of the most important part of the design process is to give the dimensions and tolerances as every part is manufactured from the dimensions given in the drawing. Therefore, it is important for every designer to understand and have a thorough knowledge of the standard practices used in industry to make sure that the information given on the drawing is correct and understood by other people. Besides dimensioning, tolerancing is equally important, especially in the assembled parts. Tolerances and fits determine how the parts will fit. Incorrect tolerances may result in a product that is not functional.

In addition to dimensioning and tolerancing, the function and the relationship that exists between the mating parts is important for the part to perform the way it was designed. This aspect of the design process is addressed by Geometric Dimensioning and tolerancing, generally known as GDT. Geometric Dimensioning and Tolerancing is a means to design and manufacture parts with respect to actual function and relationship that exists between different features of the same part or the features of the mating parts. Therefore, a good design is not achieved by just giving dimensions and tolerances. The designer has to go beyond dimensioning and think in terms of what is the intended function of the part and how the features of the parts are going to effect that function. For example, the drawing of · Figure 7-53(a) shows a part that has the required dimensions and tolerances. However, in this drawing there is no mention about the relationship that exists between the pin and the plate. In other words, there is not mention if the pin is perpendicular to the plate. If it is, to what degree should it be perpendicular. Also, it does not mention the surface with which the perpendicularity of the pin is to be measured. A design like this is open to individual interpretation based on one's intuition and experience. This is where Geometric Dimensioning and Tolerancing plays an important part in the product design process.

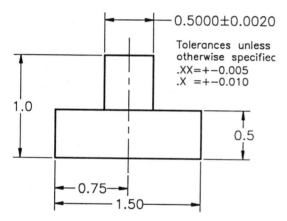

Figure 7-53(a) Using traditional dimensioning and tolerancing technique

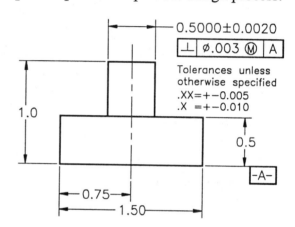

Figure 7-54(b) Using geometrical dimensioning and tolerancing

The drawing, Figure 7-54(b) has been dimensioned using Geometrical Dimensioning and Tolerancing. The feature symbols define the datum (reference plane) and the permissible deviation in the perpendicularity of the pin with respect to the bottom surface. In a drawing like this, the chances of committing a mistake is minimized. Before discusing the application of AutoCAD commands in Geometrical Dimensioning and Tolerancing, it is important to understand the following feature symbols and tolerancing components.

GEOMETRIC CHARACTERISTICS AND SYMBOLS

The following is a list of the geometric Characteristics and Symbols used in Geometrical Dimensioning and Tolerancing. These symbols are the building blocks of Geometrical Dimensioning and Tolerancing.

KIND OF FEATURE	TYPE OF FEATURE	CHARACTERISTICS	
INDIVIDUAL	FORM	Straightness	—
		Flatness	▱
		Circularity	○
		Cylindricity	⌀
INDIVIDUAL or RELATED	PROFILE	Profile of a line	⌒
		Profile of a surface	⌓
RELATED	ORIENTATION	Angularity	∠
		Perpendicularity	⊥
		Parallelism	//
	LOCATION	Position	⊕
		Concentricity	◎
		Symmetry	≡
	RUNOUT	Cicular runout	↗
		Total runout	↗↗

Figure 7-55 Geometric characteristics and symbols used in Geometrical
Dimensioning and Tolerancing

GEOMETRIC TOLERANCE COMPONENTS

The following is the list of the geometric tolerance components and Figure 7-56 shows their placement in the tolerance frame.

Feature control frame
Geometric characteristic symbol
Tolerance value
Tolerance zone descriptor
Material condition modifier
Datums

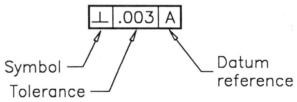

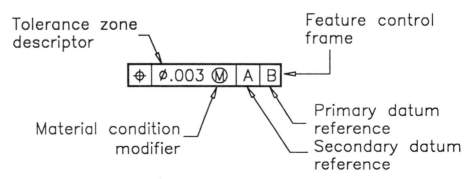

Figure 7-56 Components of Geometric tolerance

Feature Control Frame

The feature control frame is a rectangular box that contains the geometric characteristics symbols and tolerance definition. The box is automatically drawn to standard specifications and you do not need to specify the size of the box.

Geometrical Characteristics Symbol

The Geometric Characteristics Symbol indicates the characteristics of the feature. For example, straightness, flatness or perpendicularity describe the characteristic of a feature. These symbols can be picked from the Symbol dialogue box. This dialogue box is be invoked from the pull-down menu (Select Draw/ Dimensioning /Tolerance...) or by entering TOL command at AutoCAD Command: prompt. You can also access this dialogue box by selecting the SYM box in the "Geometric Tolerance" dialogue box.

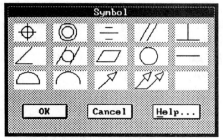

Figure 7-57 The Symbol dialogue box

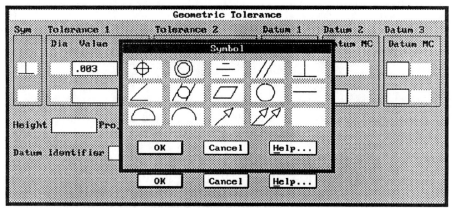

Figure 7-58 The Geometric Tolerance dialogue box

Tolerance Value and Tolerance Zone Descriptor

The Tolerance Value specifies the tolerance on the feature as indicated by the tolerance zone descriptor. For example, if the value is .003, it indicates that the feature must be within 0.003 tolerance zone. Similarly, ϕ.003 indicates that this feature must be located at true position within 0.003 diameter. The tolerance value can be entered in the value edit box of "Geometric Tolerance" dialogue box. The Tolerance Zone Descriptor can be selected by picking the box labelled Dia. This dialogue box is invoked by selecting the OK button in the "Symbol" dialogue box.

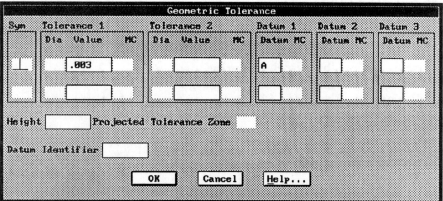

Figure 7-59 The Geometric Tolerance dialogue box

Material Condition Modifier

The Material Condition Modifier specifies the material condition when the tolerance value takes effect. For example, $\phi.003(M)$ indicates that this feature must be located at true position within 0.003 diameter at maximum material condition (MMC). The Material Condition Modifier symbol can be selected from the "Material Condition" dialogue box. This

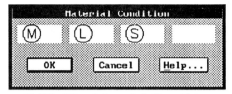

Figure 7-60 The Material Condition dialogue box

dialogue box can be invoked by selecting the MC button located just below MC in the "Geometric Tolerance" dialogue box

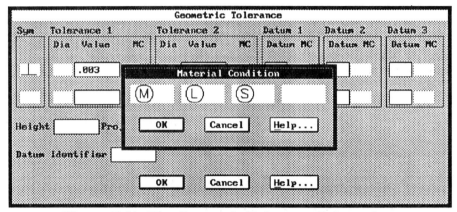

Figure 7-61 The Geometric Tolerance dialogue box

Datums

The Datum is the origin, surface, or feature from which the measurements are made. The datum is also used to establish the geometric characteristics of a feature. The Datum feature symbol consists of a reference character enclosed in feature control frame. You can create the datum feature symbol by entering charters (-A-) in the Datum edit box and then selecting a point where you want to establish that datum.

You can also combine datum references with the geometric characteristics. In the feature control frame, AutoCAD automatically positions the datum references on the right end of the feature control frame.

Example 3

In the following example you will create a feature control frame to require a perpendicularity specification.

Step 1
Use the TOLERANCE command to display the Symbol dialogue box. Select the perpendicularity symbol in the dialogue box and then select the OK button to display the Geometric Tolerance dialogue box.

Step 2
The perpendicularity symbol will be displayed in the Symbol edit box on the first row of the Geometric Tolerance dialogue box. Select the

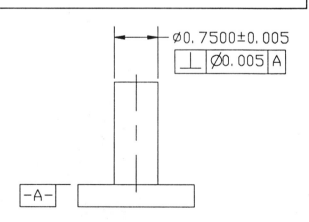

Figure X-62 Drawing for Example 3

DIA edit box in the Tolerance 1 area on the first row. A diameter symbol will appear to denote a cylindrical tolerance zone.

Step 3
Select the VALUE edit box in the Tolerance 1 area on the first row and enter 0.005.

Step 4
Select the DATUM edit box in the Datum 1 area on the first row and enter A.

Step 5
Select the OK button to accept the changes to the Geometric Tolerance dialogue box and then select a point to insert the frame. This point will be the middle left point of the frame.

Step 6
Now to place the datum symbol. Use the TOLERANCE command to display the Symbol dialogue box. Select the OK button to display the Geometric Tolerance dialogue box. Select the DATUM IDENTIFIER edit box and enter -A-.

Step 7
Select the OK button to accept the changes to the Geometric Tolerance dialogue box and then select a point to insert the frame. This point will be the upper left point of the frame.

COMPLEX FEATURE CONTROL FRAMES

Combining Geometric Characteristic
Sometimes, it is not possible to specify all geometric characteristics in one frame. For example, in Figure 7-63 show the drawing of a plate with a hole in the center. In this part it is determined that the surface C must be perpendicular to the surfaces A and B within 0.002 and 0.004 respectively. Therefore we need two frames to specify the geometric characteristics of the surface C. The first frame specifies the allowable deviation in perpendicularity of surface C with respect to surface A. The second frame specifies the allowable deviation in perpendicularity of surface C with respect to surface B. In addition to these two frames, we need a third frame that identifies the datum surface C.

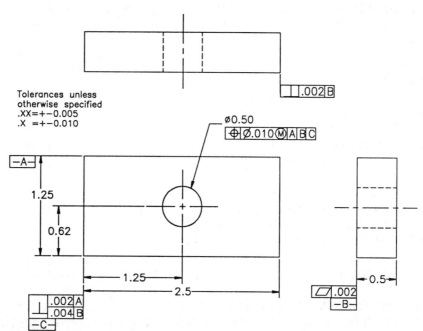

Figure 7-63 Combining feature control frames with different geometric characteristic

To create these three feature control frames, each frame has to be defined separately. These three frames can be created as follows:

1. To create the first frame, enter TOL command to invoke the "Symbol" dialogue box. Select the perpendicular symbol and then select the OK button from this dialogue box. AutoCAD will display the "Geometric Tolerance" dialogue box.

2. Enter the geometric characteristics and the datum reference in the "Geometric Tolerance" dialogue box. Once you are done entering the values, select the OK button.

3. Select the point where you want to insert the frame.

4. To create the second and third frames, repeat the above steps (1 through 3) and specify the values that must appear in this frame. In the Datum Identifier edit box enter -C- and then select the OK button to exit the dialogue box.

The third frame can also be created as follows:

1. To create the third frame, select the OK button in the "Symbol" dialogue box. AutoCAD will display the "Geometric Tolerance" dialogue box.

2. In this dialogue box, enter the letter C with dashes (-C-) in the Datum 1 column. Select the OK button and position the frame just below the second frame. You can also create the second and third frame by making a copy of the first frame and then using the DDEDIT command to edit the values. When you select the frame to be edited, AutoCAD displays the "Geometric Tolerance" dialogue box on the screen. You can enter the new values and then select the OK button to update the selected feature control frame.

Composite Position Tolerancing

Sometimes, the accuracy required within a pattern is more important than the location of the pattern with the datum surfaces. To specify such a condition, composite position tolerancing may be used. For example, the drawing in Figure 7-64 show four holes (pattern) of diameter 0.15. The design allows a maximum tolerance of 0.025 with respect to datum A, B, and C at the Maximum Material Condition (Holes are smallest). The designer wants to maintain a closer positional tolerance (0.010 at MMC) between the holes within the pattern. To specify this requirement, the designer must insert the second frame to specify this requirement. This is generally known as Composite Position Tolerancing. AutoCAD provides the facility to create the two Composite Position Tolerance frames by using the "Geometric Tolerance" dialogue box. The Composite Tolerance Frames can be created as follows:

1. Enter the TOL command to invoke the "Symbol" dialogue box. Select the position symbol and then select the OK button from this dialogue box. AutoCAD will display the "Geometric Tolerance" dialogue box.

2. In the first row of the "Geometric Tolerance" dialogue box, enter the geometric characteristics and the datum references as required for the first position tolerance frame.

3. In the second row of the "Geometric Tolerance" dialogue box, enter the geometric characteristics and the datum references as required for the second position tolerance frame.

4. Once you are done entering the values, select the OK button in the "Geometric Tolerance" dialogue box and then select the point where you want to insert the frames. AutoCAD will create the two frames and automatically align them with common position symbol as shown in Figure 7-64.

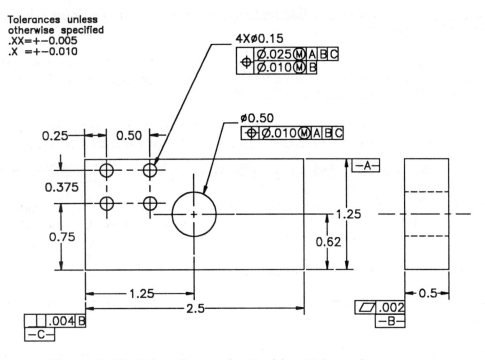

Figure 7-64 Using Composite Position Tolerancing

Projected Tolerance Zone

The drawing in Figure 7-65 shows two parts that are joined with a bolt. The lower part is threaded and the top part has a drilled hole. When these two parts are joined together, the bolt that is threaded in the lower part will have the orientation error that exists in the threaded hole. In other words, the error in the threaded hole will extend beyond the part thickness that might cause interference and the parts may not assemble.

To avoid this problem, projected tolerance is used. The projected tolerance establishes a tolerance zone that extends above the surface. In the drawing of Figure 7-65, the position tolerance for the threaded hole is 0.010 that extends 0.25 above the surface (datum A). By using the projected tolerance, you can ensure that the bolt is within the tolerance zone up to the specified distance.

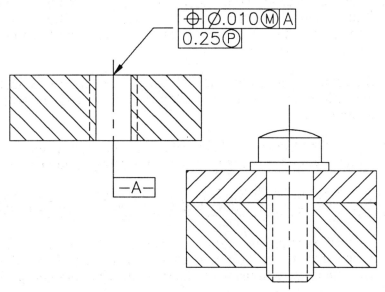

Figure 7-65 Using Composite Position Tolerancing

You can use AutoCAD's GDT feature to create Feature Control Frames for Projected Tolerance Zone as follows:

1. Enter the TOL command to invoke the "Symbol" dialogue box. Select the position symbol and then select the OK button from this dialogue box. AutoCAD will display the "Geometric Tolerance" dialogue box.

2. In the first row of the "Geometric Tolerance" dialogue box, enter the geometric characteristics and the datum references as required for the first position tolerance frame.

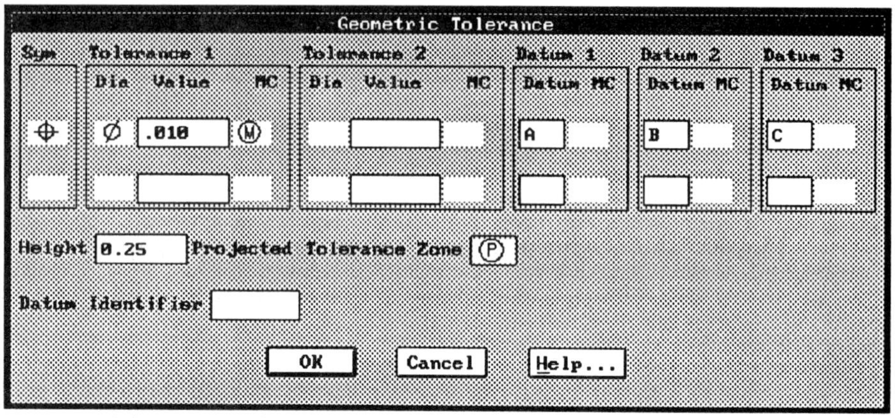

Figure 7-66 The Geometric Tolerance dialogue box

3. In the Height edit box, enter the height of the tolerance zone (0.25 for the given drawing) and pick the edit box that is to the right of Projected Tolerance Zone. The Projected Tolerance Zone symbol will be displayed in the box.

4. Once you are done entering the values, select the OK button in the "Geometric Tolerance" dialogue box and then select the point where you want to insert the frames. AutoCAD will create the two frames and automatically align them as shown in Figure 7-66.

USING FEATURE CONTROL FRAMES WITH LEADER

The Leader command has the Tolerance option that allows you to create the Feature Control Frame and attach it to the end of the leader extension line. The following is the command prompt sequence for using Leader command with Tolerance option:

Command: **LEADER**
From point: *Select a point where you want the arrow (P1)*
To point (Format/Annotatio/Undo) < Annotation >: *Select a point (P2)*
To point (Format/Annotatio/Undo) < Annotation >: *Select a point (P3)*
To point (Format/Annotatio/Undo) < Annotation >: ⏎
Annotation (or RETURN for options): ⏎
Tolerance/Copy/Block/None/ < Mtext >: **T**

When you select the Tolerance (T) option, AutoCAD will display the "Symbol" dialogue box. Select the desired symbol and then pick the OK button to invoke the "Dimension Tolerance" dialogue box. Enter the required values and select the OK button to exit the dialogue box. The Feature Control Frame with the defined geometric characteristics will be inserted at the end of the extension line as shown in Figure 7-67.

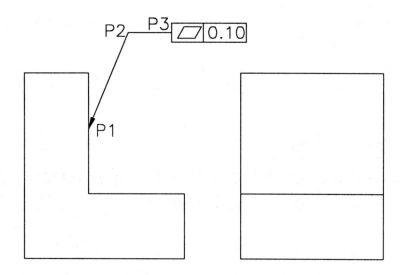

Figure 7-67 Using Feature Control Frame with leader

Example 4

In the following example you will create a leader with a combination feature control frame to control runout and cylindricity.

Step 1
Use the LEADER command to begin placing the control frame. AutoCAD will prompt you with From point: select a point where you want the tip of the arrow to be placed. AutoCAD will prompt you with To point: select a point where the first bend in the leader line will be placed. AutoCAD will prompt you with To point: select a point where the middle left side of the control frame will be placed.

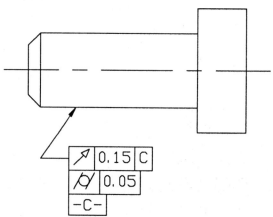

Step 2
Figure X-68 Drawing for Example 4

AutoCAD will again prompt you with To point: press RETURN to select the default option Annotation. Press RETURN again to display the Annotation options. Enter T to display the Symbol dialogue box.

Step 3
Select the runout symbol in the dialogue box and then select the OK button to display the Geometric Tolerance dialogue box.

Step 4
The runout symbol will be displayed in the Symbol edit box on the first row of the Geometric Tolerance dialogue box. Select the VALUE edit box in the Tolerance 1 area on the first row and enter 0.15.

Step 5
Select the DATUM edit box in the Datum 1 area on the first row and enter C.

Step 6
Select the SYM edit box on the second row of the Geometric Tolerance dialogue box to display the Symbol dialogue box. Select the cylindricity symbol in the dialogue box and then select the OK button to display the Geometric Tolerance dialogue box.

Step 7
The cylindricity symbol will be displayed in the Symbol edit box on the second row of the Geometric Tolerance dialogue box. Select the VALUE edit box in the Tolerance 1 area on the second row and enter 0.05.

Step 8
Select the DATUM IDENTIFIER edit box and enter -C-.

Step 9
Select the OK button to accept the changes to the Geometric Tolerance dialogue box and the control frames will be drawn in place.

EXERCISES

Exercises 4 through 9

Make the drawings as shown in the following figures (Figure 7-69 through Figure 7-75). You must create dimension style files and specify values for different dimension types like linear, radial, diameter, and ordinate. Assume the missing dimensions.

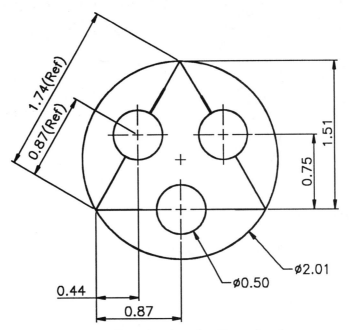

Figure 7-69 Drawing for Exercise 4

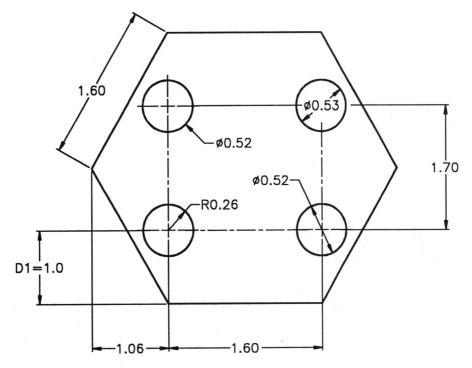

Figure 7-70 Drawing for Exercise 5

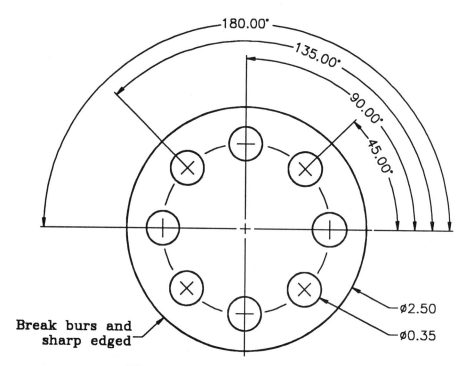

Figure 7-71 Drawing for Exercise 6

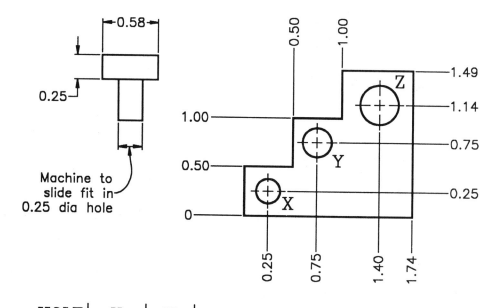

HOLE	X	Y	Z
RAD.	0.125	0.15	0.20

Figure 7-72 Drawing for Exercise 7

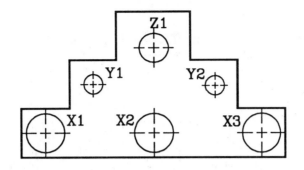

HOLE	X1	X2	X3	Y1	Y2	Z1
DIM.	R0.2	R0.2	R0.2	R0.1	R0.1	R0.15
QTY.	1	1	1	1	1	1
X	0.25	1.375	2.50	0.75	2.0	1.375
Y	0.25	0.25	0.25	0.75	0.75	1.125
Z	THRU	THRU	THRU	1.0	1.0	THRU

Figure 7-73 Drawing for Exercise 8

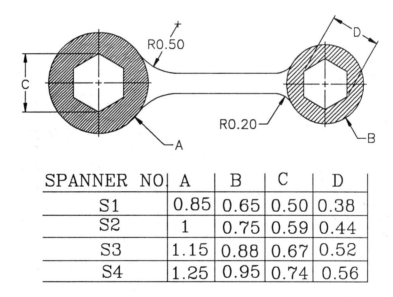

SPANNER NO.	A	B	C	D
S1	0.85	0.65	0.50	0.38
S2	1	0.75	0.59	0.44
S3	1.15	0.88	0.67	0.52
S4	1.25	0.95	0.74	0.56

Figure 7-74 Drawing for Exercise 9

Exercise 10

Draw the following figure and then use the TOL and LEADER commands to draw the geometric tolerances as shown.

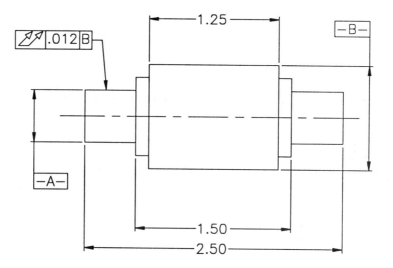

Figure 7-75 Drawing for Exercise 10

Windows Menu Customization
Solids
Rendering

8

MENU FEATURES FOR WINDOWS

If you are using AutoCAD for Windows, you have additional menu features available to you that are not available on DOS. For example, in Windows you can write partial menus, toolbar and accelerator key definitions. After writing the menus, AutoCAD lets you load the menu and use it with the standard menu. For example, you could load a partial menu and use it like a pull-down menu. You can also unload the menus that you do not want to use. These features make it easier to use the menus that have been developed by AutoCAD users and developers.

Loading Menus

When you load a menu file in Windows, AutoCAD generates the following files:

.mnc and **.mnr** file   When you load a menu file (**.mnu**), AutoCAD compiles the menu file and creates **.mnc** and **.mnr** files. The **.mnc** file is a compiled menu file like **.mnx** file for DOS. The **.mnr** file contains the bitmaps used by the menu.

.mns file   When you load the menu file, AutoCAD also creates a **.mns** file. This is an ASCII file that is same as **.mnu** file when you initially load the menu file. Each time you make a change in the contents of the file, AutoCAD changes the **.mns** file.

.ini file   This file contains information about the toolbar position. For example, when you load a menu the initial position is defined in the menu file. However, when you make changes in the position of a tool bar, for example when you dock a toolbar or change the floating status, the new position is recorded in the **.ini** file.

The **.mns** file is used as a source file for creating **.mnc** and **.mnr** files. If you make a change in the menu file (**.mnu**) after the **.mns** file is created, you must delete the **.mns** and **.mnc** files before you load the new menu. Otherwise, AutoCAD will not recognize the changes you made in the menu file.

Menu Section Labels

The following is a list of the menu section labels:

Section label	Description
***MENUGROUP	Menu file group name
***TOOLBARS	Toolbar definition
***HELPSTRING	
***ACCELERATORS	Accelerator key definitions

99

Example 1

In this example you will write a partial menu file for Windows. The menu file should have two pull-down menus as shown in the figure.

Step 1
Use a text editor to write the following menu file. You can also use AutoCAD's EDIT function to invoke the DOS editor. The name of the file is assumed to be MENU1.MNU.

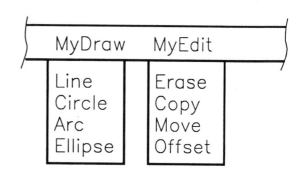

Figure 8-1 Pull-down menus

Command: **EDIT**
File to edit: **MENU1.MNU**   *(Enter the name of the file)*

The following is the listing of the menu file for this example.

```
***MENUGROUP=Menu1                          1
***POP1                                     2
[/MMyDraw]                                  3
[/LLine]^C^CLine                            4
[/CCircle]^C^CCircle                        5
[/AArc]^C^CArc                              6
[/EEllipse]^C^CEllipse                      7

***POP2                                     8
[/MMyEdit]                                  9
[/EErase]^C^CErase                          10
[/CCopy]^C^CCopy                            11
[/MMove]^C^CMove                            12
[/OOffset]^C^COffset                        13
```

Explanation

Line 1
***MENUGROUP=Menu1
MENUGROUP is the section label and the **Menu1** is the name-tag for the menu group. This is called the Menugroup. The name of the Menugroup can be up to 32 characters long (alpha-numeric), excluding spaces. There is only one Menugroup in a menu file. All section labels must be preceded by *******.

Line 2
***POP1
POP1 is the pull-down menu section label and the items on line numbers 3 through 7 belong to this section. Similarly, the items on line numbers 9 through 13 belong to the pull down menu section **POP2**.

Line 3
[/MMyDraw]
/M defines the **mnemonic** key, that you can use to activate the menu item. For example, **/M** will display a dash under the letter **M** in the text string that follows it. If you enter the letter

M, AutoCAD will execute the command defined in the menu item. **MyDraw** is the menu item label. The text string inside the brackets **[   ]** , except /M, has no function. They are used for displaying the function name so that the user can recognize the command that will be executed by selecting that item.

Line 4
[/LLine]^C^CLine
In this line, the /L defines the mnemonic key and the **Line** that is inside the brackets is the menu item label. **^C^C** cancels the command twice and the **Line** is AutoCAD's LINE command. The part of the menu item statement that outside the brackets is executed when you select an item from the menu. When you select this item, AutoCAD will execute the LINE command.

Step 2
Save the file and then load the menu file using AutoCAD's MENULOAD command.

Command: **MENULOAD**

When you enter MENULOAD command, AutoCAD displays the **Menu Customization** dialogue box on the screen. To load the menu file, enter the name of the menu file, MENU1.MNU in the **File Name:** edit box. You can also use the Browse option to invoke **Select Menu File** dialogue box. Select the name of the file and then use the OK button to return to **Menu Customization** dialogue box. To load the selected menu file pick the **LOAD** button. To exit the **Menu Customization** dialogue box, select the **Close** button.

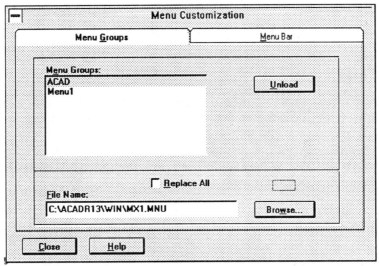

Figure 8-2 Menu Customization dialogue box

You can also load the menu file from the command line as follows

Command: **FILEDIA**
New value for FILEDIA <1>: **0**   *(Disables the file dialogue boxes)*

Command: **MENULOAD**
Menu file name or . for none <acad.mnc>: **MENU1.MNU**

Step 3
Once the menu is loaded, use the MENUCMD (AutoLISP function) to display the partial menus.

Command: **(MENUCMD "P8=+MENU1.POP1")**
Command: **(MENUCMD "P9=+MENU1.POP2")**

After entering these commands, AutoCAD will display the pull-down menu titles in the menu bar as shown in the figure. If you select MyDraw, the corresponding pull-down menu as defined in the menu file will be displayed on the screen. Similarly, selecting MyEdit will display the corresponding edit pull-down menu.

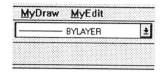

Figure 8-3 MENUCMD command places the menu titles in the menu bar

MENUCMD is an AutoLISP function and P8 determines where the POP1 menu will be displayed. You can position it anywhere in the menu bar. MENU1 is the Menugroup name as defined in the menu file and POP1 is the pull-down menu section label. The Menugroup name and the menu section label must be separated by a period (.).

Step 4

If you need to unload the partial menu file, enter the MENULOAD or MENUUNLOAD command to invoke the **Menu Customization** dialogue box. AutoCAD will display the names of the menu files in the Menu Groups: list box. Select the **Menu1** menu file and then select the **Unload** file. AutoCAD will unload the menu file. Select the **Close** button to exit the dialogue box.

You can also unload the menu file from the command line as follows.

Command: **FILEDIA**
New value for FILEDIA <1>: **0**

Command: **MENUUNLOAD**
Enter the name of the MENUGROUP to unload: **MENU1.MNU**

Accelerator Keys

AutoCAD for Windows also supports user defined accelerator keys. For example, if you enter C at Command: prompt, AutoCAD draws a circle. You cannot use the C key to enter the COPY command. To use the C key for entering COPY command, you can define the accelerator keys. You can combine the Shift key with C in the menu file so that when you hold down the shift key and then press C key, AutoCAD will execute the copy command. The following file is the listing of a menu file that uses the accelerator keys.

```
***MENUGROUP=Menu1
***POP1
**Alias
[/MMyDraw]
[/LLine]^C^CLine
[/CCircle]^C^CCircle
[/AArc]^C^CArc
ID_Ellipse [/EEllipse]^C^CEllipse

***POP2
[/MMyEdit]
[/EErase]^C^CErase
ID_Copy [/CCopy]^C^CCopy
[/OOffset]^C^COffset
[/VMove]^C^CMov

***ACCELERATORS
ID_Ellipse [CONTROL+"E"]
ID_Copy [SHIFT+"C"]
```

```
[CONTROL"Q"]^C^CQuit
```

This menu file defines three accelerator keys. The **ID_Copy [SHIFT + "C"]** accelerator key consists of two parts. The ID_Copy is the name tag that must be the same as used earlier in the menu item definition. The SHIFT + "C" is the label that contains the modifier (SHIFT) and the key name (C). The key name or the string like "Escape" must be enclosed in quotation marks. After you load the file, Shift+C will enter the COPY command and Ctrl+E will draw an ellipse. Similarly, Ctrl+Q will cancel the existing command and enter QUIT command.

Toolbars

The contents of the toolbar and its default layout can be specified in the Toolbar section of the menu file. Each toolbar must be defined in a separate submenu. The following is the general format of the toolbar definition:

```
***TOOLBARS
**MYTOOLS1
Tag1 [Toolbar ("Toolbarname", Orient, Visible, XVal,YVal, Rows)]
Tag2 [Button ("Buttonname", ID_Small, ID_Large,)]Macro
Tag3 [Flyout ("Flyoutname",ID_Small, ID_Large, Icon, Alias)]Macro
Tag4 [Control (Element)]
```

The following menu file contains a sample toolbar for Line command:

```
***MENUGROUP=Menu1
***POP1
**Alias
[/MMyDraw]
[/LLine]^C^CLine
[/CCircle]^C^CCircle
[/AArc]^C^CArc
ID_Ellipse [/EEllipse]^C^CEllipse

***POP2
[/MMyEdit]
[/EErase]^C^CErase
ID_Copy [/CCopy]^C^CCopy
[/OOffset]^C^COffset
[/VMove]^C^CMov

***ACCELERATORS
ID_Copy [SHIFT+"C"]
ID_Ellipse [CONTROL+"E"]
[CONTROL"Q"]^C^CQuit
[CONTROLSHIFT"S"]^C^CSaveas

***TOOLBARS
**TB_LINE
ID_TbLine [_Toolbar("Line",_Floating,_Show, 10, 120 ,1)]
ID_Line[_Button("Line",ICON_16_LINE,ICON_32_LINE)]^C^C_Line
```

SOLIDS

The following is the command summary of Solids related commands:

Old Command Names	New Command Names	Old Command Names	New Command Names
Draw Commands		**Editing Commands**	
	REGION	SOLUNION	UNION
	AMECONVERT	SOLSUB	SUBTRACT
	ACISIN	SOLINT	INTERSECT
SOLBOX	BOX	SOLCHAM	CHAMFER
SOLCONE	CONE	SOLFIL	FILLET
SOLCYL	CYLINDER	SOLCUT	SLICE
SOLREV	REVOLVE		
SOLSPHERE	SPHERE		
SOLTORUS	TORUS		
SOLWEDGE	WEDGE		

Old Command Names	New Command Names
Inquiry Commands	
SOLMASSP	MASSPROP
SOLSECT	SECTION
SOLINTERF	INTERFERE
	STLOUT

Following are some examples of SOLID commands.

MASSPROP

```
----------------------- SOLIDS ------------------
Mass:        26.97775
Volume:      26.97775

Bounding box:        X: -2.5000 -- 2.0010
                     Y: -2.5000 -- 2.5000
                     Z: -0.7500 -- 3.0000

Centroid:            X: -0.0623
                     Y: 0.0001
                     Z: 0.6068

Moments of inertia:  X: 74.3905
                     Y: 71.0374
                     Z: 60.9835
Products of inertia: XY: -0.0001
                     YZ: 0.0018
                     ZX: 0.6331

Radii of gyration:   X: 1.6606
                     Y: 1.6227
                     Z: 1.5035

Principal moments and X-Y-Z directions about centroid:
            I: 65.1039 along [0.9313 0.0001,-0.3644]
            J: 60.9993 along [-0.0004 1.0000 -0.0009]
            K: 60.2320 along [0.3644 0.0010 0.9313]

Write to a file ? <N> : ◄⟶
```

SLICE

Command: **SLICE**
Select objects: **(Select the solid)**
Select objects: ←┘
1 solid selected.
Slicing plane by Object/Zaxis/View/XY/YZ/ZX/ < 3points > : **XY**
Point on XY plane < 0,0,0 > : ←┘
Both sides/ < Point on desired side of the plane > : **(Select point F using ENDpoint O'Snap)**

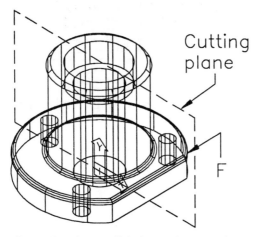

Figure 8-4 Cutting solid through XY plane

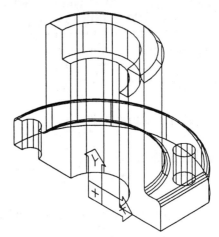

Figure 8-5 Solid after cutting

SECTION

Command: **SECTION**
Select objects: **(Select the solid)**
Select objects: ←┘
Sectioning plane by Object/Zaxis/View/XY/YZ/ZX/ < 3points > : **XY**
Point on XY plane < 0,0,0 > : ←┘

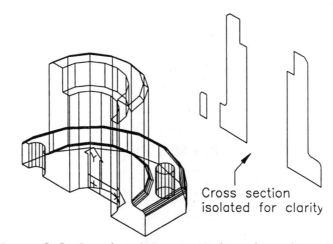

Figure 8-6 Creating the cross section of a solid

RENDERING ENHANCEMENTS

Following are some of the AutoCAD Release 13 Render enhancements:

1. Faster new rendering engine for Gouraud and Phong render.
2. More options in dialogue user interface for rendering to a file.
3. Spotlight feature has been added.
4. The lights can be colored.
5. The reflection color can be user defined.
6. The materials in blocks can be attached.
7. It is easier to use interface.
8. 3D Studio files input and output.
9. The material library and the material editor have dialogue user interface.

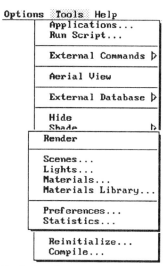

Figure 8-7 Selecting Render from Tools pull-down menu

Render Dialogue Boxes

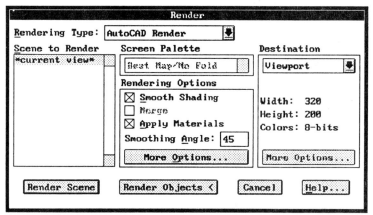

Figure 8-8 Render dialogue box

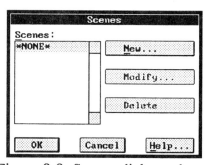

Figure 8-8 Scenes dialogue box

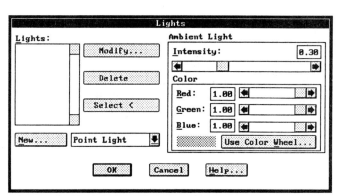

Figure 8-10 Lights dialogue box

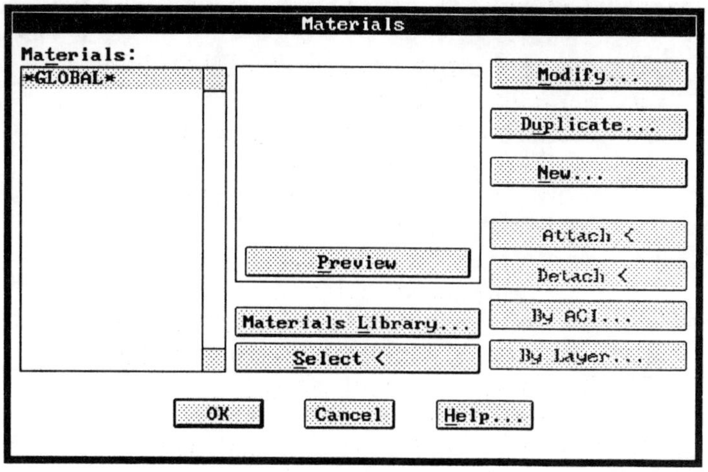

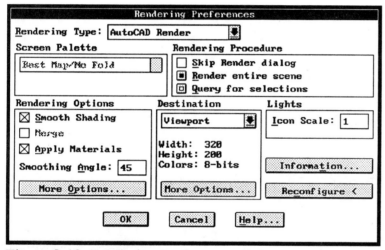

Figure 8-11 Materials Library dialogue box

Figure 8-12 Rendering Preferences dialogue box

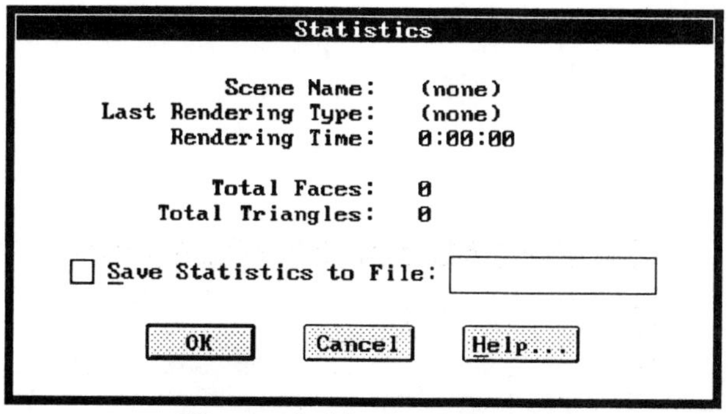

Figure 8-13 Statistics dialogue box

-Notes-

-Notes-

-Notes-

-Notes-

-Notes-

-Notes-

-Notes-

910